THE 101 HABITS OF HIGHLY SUCCESSFUL

SCREEN WRITERS

2ND EDITION

INSIDER SECRETS FROM HOLLYWOOD'S TOP WRITERS

KARL IGLESIAS

Avon, Massachusetts

DEDICATION

To all aspiring screenwriters who sacrifice so much to share their souls through the screenplay.

May these 101 habits be the seeds that inspire your next masterpiece.

• • •

Published by
Adams Media, a division of F+W Media, Inc.
57 Littlefield Street, Avon, MA 02322. U.S.A.
www.adamsmedia.com

ISBN 10: 1-4405-2789-X
ISBN 13: 978-1-4405-2789-0
eISBN 10: 1-4405-2856-X
eISBN 13: 978-1-4405-2856-9

Printed in the United States of America.

10 9 8 7 6 5 4 3 2

Library of Congress Cataloging-in-Publication Data
is available from the publisher.

This publication is designed to provide accurate and authoritative information with regard to the subject matter covered. It is sold with the understanding that the publisher is not engaged in rendering legal, accounting, or other professional advice. If legal advice or other expert assistance is required, the services of a competent professional person should be sought.
—From a *Declaration of Principles* jointly adopted by a Committee of the American Bar Association and a Committee of Publishers and Associations

Many of the designations used by manufacturers and sellers to distinguish their product are claimed as trademarks. Where those designations appear in this book and Adams Media was aware of a trademark claim, the designations have been printed with initial capital letters.

This book is available at quantity discounts for bulk purchases.
For information, please call 1-800-289-0963.

ACKNOWLEDGMENTS

While most of the words in this book belong to the screenwriters interviewed for this project, it is clear where my appreciation lies. First and foremost, a heartfelt thank you and deep appreciation must go to those twenty-two screenwriters for granting me their time and energy despite their hectic Hollywood schedules, and for their willingness to share their knowledge and experience with the reader. They are, in alphabetical order: Ron Bass, Steven de Souza, Gerald DiPego, Leslie Dixon, Tony Gilroy, Akiva Goldsman, Derek Haas & Michael Brandt, Amy Holden Jones, Laeta Kalogridis, Nicholas Kazan, Jim Kouf, Andrew W. Marlowe, Bill Marsilii, Aline Brosh McKenna, Scott Rosenberg, Terry Rossio, Eric Roth, Michael Schiffer, Tom Schulman, Ed Solomon, and Robin Swicord. Your insightful comments are the soul of this book.

Special thanks to Victoria Sandbrook and Jennifer Lawler for their helpful comments and editorial support.

And to my friends and family, especially Tara, Allie, and Aaron, for their caring and support.

CONTENTS

PART 2   CREATIVITY: Summoning the Muse

PART 3 DISCIPLINE: Applying the Seat of Your Pants to the Seat of the Chair

PART 4 STORYCRAFT: Weaving a Great Tale

PART 5   MARKETING: It's Not Who You Know, It's Your Writing

PART 6 THE FOUR PS: Patience, Perseverance, Passion, and Practice

HABIT n. 1. a. A recurrent, often unconscious pattern of behavior that is acquired through frequent repetition. b. An established disposition of the mind or character. 2. Customary manner or practice: a person of ascetic habits. 3. An addiction.

—THE AMERICAN HERITAGE DICTIONARY
OF THE ENGLISH LANGUAGE, THIRD EDITION

• • •

The secret to success in any field is to find what successful people do, think about and act on, and do the same.

—ANTHONY ROBBINS

INTRODUCTION

FADE IN

We are what we repeatedly do.
Excellence, then, is not an act, but a habit.
—ARISTOTLE

Despite the old adage attributed to William Goldman, "Nobody knows anything," there's one thing every studio executive knows for sure: It all starts with a great script.

But most scripts are terrible, mediocre, by the numbers, or almost good, which means that in order to feed the industry's ravenous appetite, executives are *desperately* looking for great material.

If you want something you've never had,
you have to do something you've never done!
—KIMNESHA BENNS

The problem isn't craft. It's the temperament of aspiring writers—their traits, skills, talents, and habits—that keeps them from writing great screenplays. It may sound harsh, but the sad truth is that more than half of the scripts currently making the rounds in Hollywood were written by writers who have no business being screenwriters. Sure, everyone goes to the movies and knows when they're good or bad, and everyone has access to a computer with which to write their screenplay. But think about this: Everyone can recognize a funny joke, but can everyone create one that's as funny and has never been told before?

There's a multimillion-dollar business devoted entirely to giving outdated prescriptions, rules, and formulas to aspiring screenwriters—in an industry that frowns on formulas. Aspiring screenwriters are willing to pay anything to get that magic key that will open the door to a spec sale that will instantly change their lives. (A spec script is a screenplay written without pay, on "speculation" that it will sell to a producer or get representation by an agent.)

> *One hasn't become a writer until one has*
> *distilled writing into a habit, and that habit*
> *has been forced into an obsession.*
>
> —Niyi Osundare

In order to write a great script, you have to be a real screenwriter because, like an aged wine, it takes time and hard work to develop the necessary craft to write great scripts. You can't just be a fly-by-night hack, dreaming of the big score.

> *Winners have simply formed the habit of*
> *doing things losers don't like to do.*
>
> —Albert Gray

The difference between successful screenwriters and unsuccessful screenwriters is that successful screenwriters do all the things that unsuccessful ones want to do but can't do or don't know how to do. Modeling what works is the philosophy at the heart of every master–apprentice craft. Why not screenwriting? Someone is doing it right—many are, in fact. Why not ask them how they do it? "Hey, successful screenwriter dude, what are your habits? What works for you? Enlighten me."

> *If I wanted to become a tramp, I would seek information*
> *and advice from the most successful tramp I could find.*
> *If I wanted to become a failure, I would seek advice from*
> *people who have never succeeded. If I wanted to succeed*
> *in all things, I would look around me for those who are*
> *succeeding, and do as they have done.*
>
> —Joseph Marshall Wade

The focus of this book is not on how to write a formulaic script but on what it takes to become the writer who creates a unique one. In other words, on the habits and traits that increase the odds of your writing a great script—and also developing a successful career as a screenwriter.

What This Book Is About

The more than one hundred books on the craft of screenwriting attempt to teach the reader *what* to do, whereas this book outlines, by asking those who are already doing it successfully, *how* to do it. It focuses on the necessary habits, so that the "how" becomes second nature to you. It's based on the simple philosophy of modeling excellence and the common sense approach of the apprentice–master relationship.

This book departs from the established interview books in that its structure is organized by topic rather than by individual interview, following a much more efficient model of reverse engineering. In other words, it focuses on a particular habit, trait, or indispensable skill, and then has a group of highly successful screenwriters share their thoughts on the subject, much like a panel of experts discussing a specific topic.

The habits presented here are simple. They're just habits of action and thought. Many will seem obvious, but they bear repeating because aspiring screenwriters often ignore them. Others are surprising and sometimes even shocking. By themselves, they may not make you a successful writer. But developing new habits and combining them with your talent will definitely make you a *better* writer. All this book can accomplish is to share with you what highly successful screenwriters believe and do on a regular basis with the hope that you will be intrigued and inspired enough to emulate them.

Since each screenwriter is unique and has habits that work for him or her, you'll notice that several habits listed seem to contradict each other. For example, the habit of rewriting after finishing the first draft conflicts with the habit of rewriting as you go along. These habits are not gospel but simply what works for each of the screenwriters featured here. It's up to you to try them out and see if they work for you.

Look at this book as an effective way to have all the interviewed screenwriters be your personal mentors. Study their habits, learn from them, and maybe their wisdom will rub off on you and arm you with enough knowledge and self-confidence to accomplish your goals.

How This Book Is Organized

What sets this book apart is its structure and its focus on the specific habits that have made some screenwriters highly successful. It is based on the simple philosophy of modeling excellence and the common sense approach of the apprentice–master relationship.

Part 1, *Passion*, discusses what makes screenwriters different from other people, their common traits and skills, and their reasons for becoming a screenwriter despite all the drawbacks. Included in this part are thoughts on believing in your talent; being committed to a career, not just one spec script; how to overcome various fears associated with the writing vocation; and learning the craft.

Part 2, *Creativity*, focuses on the creative process, how working screenwriters summon their muse to come up with fresh ideas and how they flesh out a story. It also explores their writing environments and favorite times to write.

Part 3, *Discipline*, the heart of this book, guides you through the basic components critical to success, including the writing habit and time management, and offers tips on overcoming procrastination, dealing with writer's block, and the rewriting process.

Part 4, *Storycraft*, shares insider secrets and specific tips to make each of the basic elements of a great script easier to manage, from conflict and characters to dialogue and evoking emotion on the page. It also explores what makes a great story and what differentiates good from bad writing.

Part 5, *Marketing*, focuses on the business side of screenwriting and how to market yourself as a writer, offering tips on the importance of establishing a network of supporters, mentors, and contacts in an industry that runs on relationships, from getting your first agent to pitching with enthusiasm and overcoming nervousness.

Part 6, *The Four Ps,* examines the need for patience, dealing with the Hollywood system, and keeping the dream alive, from perseverance and belief in your material to handling rejection like a pro.

Finally, a closing chapter, "Fade Out," leaves readers with final words of inspiration as they return to their favorite task, writing their next project—coming soon to a theater near you.

There's an old industry adage that in Hollywood, it's not who you know but who knows you.

I will add that it's also not what you know but what you do. It's all about action.

But we can't act until we discover the 101 habits that have made our twenty-two screenwriters successful. Let's find out who they are and how they made the leap from aspiring to professional screenwriters.

Screenwriters' Panel

Ron Bass (*A Season in Central Park, Snow Flower and the Secret Fan, Amelia, Mozart and the Whale, The Lazarus Child, Passion of Mind, Snow Falling on Cedars, Entrapment, Stepmom, What Dreams May Come, How Stella Got Her Groove Back, My Best Friend's Wedding, Waiting to Exhale, Dangerous Minds, When a Man Loves a Woman, The Joy Luck Club, Sleeping with the Enemy, Rain Man, Black Widow*)

In 1982, I made an investment that went wrong and I needed to make more money. My literary agent said he had a contact at Reader's Digest Condensed Books [who] had this idea for a World War II spy novel. If I could write up a proposal that would get his contact excited enough to make a Reader's Digest commitment to my publisher, he could get me a $20,000 advance. The thing was that I hated World War II stories. They're kind of corny, Nazi stories. So I decided to write the "Anti–World War II" story, the kind of story that could have happened anywhere, anytime, that showed that people, even Nazis, and beautiful resistance people, and American counterspies were still people, with fears and loves, dreams and hopes.

I wrote this 115-page treatment, and it sold, and I got an advance that was even bigger than expected. When the film rights were bought, I insisted on writing the screenplay. I got up at three, wrote until six, the kids got up, I spent time with them until seven, and then got to work by eight and was a good lawyer until six, had dinner with my wife, and played with the kids. All weekend long I'm writing, and on vacations I'm writing like crazy. I wrote four scripts in a year and a half while I was practicing law. And then a good friend who happened to be the head of Fox at the time said to me, "How many blind deals would you need from me to be able to quit law entirely and just write?" I thought about it, did the calculations, and it came down to two scripts. He said, "You got it." I thought about it, talked with my wife and with my partner at the firm, who was also my mentor. He said, "That's great, you're a great writer, you're making the right decision. If you ever fail or if you want to return to your old job and be a lawyer again, there'll always be a place for you here." He made it really easy to follow my calling of love.

Steven de Souza (*Blast, Knock Off, Judge Dredd, Beverly Hills Cop III, The Flintstones, Ricochet, Hudson Hawk, Die Hard 2, Die Hard, The Running Man, 48 Hrs.*)

I stumbled into my first show-biz job in Philadelphia, working at a local television station as a writer-producer. Eventually I got laid off, but through networking I managed to get from one TV station to another, did talk shows, local commercials, cooking shows, evangelist shows on Sundays. It got to a point where I couldn't take this anymore. I had all these writing samples, so I decided to go to Hollywood. I had an emotional talk with my wife because we had just had a little baby at the time, and I took a bargain basement flight to Los Angeles where I had an uncle and aunt. My aunt [had a friend who] happened to know a lawyer who had quit to become an agent. So I called him up, sent him my samples, he liked them, asked me if I'd deign to do television. I said sure, I want to work. So he gave my samples to one of his clients who was desperate for writers, and who happened to be the producer of these bionic shows at Universal. As soon as he read them, he hired me. Six days after I arrived in town, I signed a contract with Universal Studios. I was even written up in *Variety* as one of these stories that never happen: Instant success!

Of course, thirteen weeks later, I got laid off when the show got canceled. But since Universal was a television factory making most of the shows for all three networks, I got swapped around between shows like a baseball player. Someone hires you for a detective show across the hall or a little work on a lawyer show. It's a tremendous exposure to all kinds of genres and to a certain discipline because you only have seven days to make these suckers.

Paramount quickly lured me away from Universal to write pilots for them, which sold, and I had the dumb luck of being asked to write dramatic pilots. One of them was called *The Renegades,* which was Patrick Swayze's first gig, and the producer on that was Larry Gordon. One day, he calls me into a meeting, and there is Joel Silver, who was his protégé, and Michael Eisner and Jeffrey Katzenberg. They'd seen my work on these pilots under tough situations, and I had a reputation for doing action adventure with a sense of humor. So they offered me this movie they'd been developing for about six years. They said, "We need to make it funny without sabotaging the action, and we think you're the guy" And that was *48 Hrs.* So a lot of this is about being in the right place at the right time, a lot of dumb luck, working for people to whom you can prove yourself, and showing them what you can do so that when opportunities present themselves they think of you. It's not like I had some conscious plan: "*Bowling for Dollars* will lead to the *Bionic Woman* and then it's a short hop to Eddie Murphy." It just happened without me thinking about it.

Gerald DiPego (*Little Murder, The Forgotten, Angel Eyes, Instinct, Message in a Bottle, Phenomenon, Sharky's Machine*)

I was always doing some kind of writing. I was a prose writer and a reporter through college, and I took courses in film in graduate school. Ultimately they led me to making my living as an educational and industrial film writer, which are still markets most people are unaware of. I was living in Chicago doing these industrials, already freelancing for a couple of years, and I had time to develop my own spec script and, like a lot of other people, bring it with me to Hollywood, thinking I could support myself writing industrials until I got my break. My dream was not necessarily to sell it, but use it as a sample, and that's what happened eventually. I showed it to enough people that it landed, ultimately, on the right desk at the right time.

Leslie Dixon (*Tower Heist, Limitless, The Heartbreak Kid, Hairspray, Just Like Heaven, Freaky Friday, Pay It Forward, The Thomas Crown Affair, That Old Feeling, Look Who's Talking Now, Loverboy, Overboard, Outrageous Fortune*)

I had no formal education whatsoever, completely on my own from the age of eighteen, financially and every other way, working crappy jobs, playing in a bluegrass band for a while, always having some guitar boyfriend or other. And then one day I had an epiphany. I think I was twenty-three. I said to myself, "If I'm still here living this life with these people and doing this ten years from now, I'll kill myself." So in a calculated move, I decided to go to L.A. to become a screenwriter. I didn't have one extra dollar, worked crummy jobs to support myself, didn't have health insurance, drove around without car insurance, and most of the time my car didn't run so I didn't drive at all.

I couldn't afford any screenwriting classes, but I was able to get a library card at AFI [American Film Institute], which was great because I got to read great scripts that way. I probably learned more from that than a small stint at a Z-grade production company, reading all the scripts that came in. Those were so awful that it puffed up my ego and made me think I could do better than this, that I shouldn't be so intimidated. I was in L.A. for almost a year before I found an idea that was commercial enough. I actually wrote it with a friend because we were both broke, miserable, and desperate. He was very funny and I was very funny, and we thought we could make each other funnier. And we sold it. It wasn't a huge deal; people weren't making million-dollar deals then. But we were off and running. And of course, as these things go in Hollywood, we became inseparable to each other, professionally broke up, and I went my own way. One deal later, I wrote *Outrageous Fortune*.

Tony Gilroy (*The Bourne Legacy, State of Play, Duplicity, Michael Clayton, The Bourne Ultimatum, The Bourne Supremacy, The Bourne Identity, Proof of Life, Bait, Armageddon, The Devil's Advocate, Extreme Measures, Dolores Claiborne, The Cutting Edge*)

Before I started writing, I was deeply involved in music and songwriting. I also tried my hand at serious short fiction, tried to write a couple of novels, but because my father was a playwright and a screenwriter, I thought I'd give it a try. My brother was also into it. It turned out to be much more difficult than I thought. But I really liked it. That medium felt comfortable to me. But like everyone else, I wasn't very good at it at first. I was good enough that people who read my work would tell me it wasn't good enough but that I should write another one. I spent five or six years tending bar, trying very hard not to play music, which had been my life up to that point, trying to make a courageous transition to being a screenwriter, and just getting better and better at it. I became a serious student of it, writing many specs, even collaborating with my brother on a few projects.

Eventually, we wrote something that people liked. A friend had a girlfriend whose friend was a reader at New Line. He liked it but said that New Line would never make it but that he was trying to write a script, would I want to discuss the idea over drinks? So we met, and it was a cool idea for an action film and he was a really cool guy, we ended up becoming friends, so we collaborated on the script. He turned out to be really plugged in and knew everybody, so we ended up selling the script to Cannon for Guild minimum. We split the check, and I ended up meeting people through ICM [International Creative Management], who hip-pocketed me for a while until I got better.

Akiva Goldsman (*Angels & Demons, I Am Legend, The Da Vinci Code, Cinderella Man, I Robot, A Beautiful Mind, Practical Magic, Lost in Space, Batman & Robin, A Time to Kill, Batman Forever, Silent Fall, The Client*)

Before screenplays, I wrote fiction and short fiction, but mainly *unsold* fiction. I wasn't particularly good, but I was very persistent. I went to college and got a graduate degree in creative writing, got a job working with severely emotionally disturbed children, and wrote at night. During my NYU days, I was invited to take a private writing course taught by an extraordinary writing teacher, Gordon Lish. He believed there were too many loud voices out there, and unless you had a clear voice, no one could hear you, so you had to be very authentic. The class was six hours straight, with no pee breaks. Gordon believed that if you didn't have the will to control your bladder for six hours, you didn't have the will to write, which sounds fabulous in theory, but it was unbelievably agonizing. You'd get there and start reading your story aloud to the class and often you'd get no further than a sentence or two before Gordon would tear you apart in front of everyone. He'd say, "Let me tell you why this sucks," and would say it in a very articulate way, which was really painful, but the process was as much psychological as it was literary. It was shearing off all pretenses so you were forced to dig deeper and deeper and find your own voice, because it wasn't like next week you could come back with the same story. You had to write a new story every week. By the time I got to read a whole page aloud, it was a profoundly gratifying experience.

So I'd put these stories in envelopes and send them out everywhere, and I'd get these really charming rejection notes. By the time I was twenty-eight or twenty-nine, I realized I wasn't going to make it as a fiction writer and I thought, "My God, there's gotta be some way of doing this." I've always loved the movies, so I took Robert McKee's Structure class, which I highly recommend, and then I wrote a script, and I'm a bad example because it sold.

Derek Haas & Michael Brandt (*The Courier, The Double, 3:10 to Yuma, Wanted, 2 Fast 2 Furious*)

We went to college together—undergrad and grad school at Baylor University in Waco, Texas. I studied English literature and Michael studied film. We took a screenwriting class together and realized we liked the same types of films. A few years later, Michael moved to Hollywood and worked as a film editor. We started writing a script together and when we finished, Michael gave it to his post-production supervisor on a film he was working on. She gave it to a producer's assistant, who gave it to a producer, who gave it to Brad Pitt's manager, who gave it to Brad Pitt. He said he wanted to star in it and it sold. So . . . the secret to making it in Hollywood is to have Brad Pitt say he wants to star in your spec script.

Amy Holden Jones (*The Relic, The Rich Man's Wife, The Getaway* [1994], *Indecent Proposal, Beethoven, Mystic Pizza, Maid to Order, Love Letters* [1984])

My first aspirations were to be a documentary filmmaker, but I quickly found that in order to do that you had to be independently wealthy, which I wasn't. So I became a film editor until Roger Corman gave me my first chance to direct. Then I had to rewrite the script. I had to keep writing things for myself to direct. Now, I much prefer writing to directing.

Laeta Kalogridis (*Battle Angel, Shutter Island, Pathfinder, Alexander, Night Watch*)

I was in school at UCLA, the MFA program, after having been at the Texas Center for Writers at UT Austin. I sold my first script before I graduated from the UCLA program. I had written a spec script about Joan of Arc, and a friend of mine, a fellow student in the Producing Program at UCLA, introduced me to an agent who he had worked with. The agent liked the script, and he was able to sell it to Joel Silver at Warner Brothers.

Nicholas Kazan (*Enough, Bicentennial Man, Homegrown, Fallen, Matilda, Dream Lover, Mobsters, Reversal of Fortune, Patty Hearst, At Close Range, Frances*)

I started by writing plays in college, and wrote them primarily for about seven years. The last two years of that, I began writing screenplays because I was always obsessed with movies, and I did that for about five years full-time with very little success. And then one day, I wrote a screenplay in a completely different way. It was almost all images, and I used the images rather than the dialogue for dramatic effect. For me, that was the real transition from playwriting to screenwriting.

Jim Kouf (*Money for Nothing, National Treasure, Taxi, Snow Dogs, Rush Hour, Gang Related, Operation Dumbo Drop, Another Stakeout, Disorganized Crime, Stakeout, Miracles, Secret Admirer, Shaker Run, American Dreamer, Class, Up the Creek*)

I took a date to see an exclusive engagement of *The Wild Bunch*. I walked out stunned by what I'd just seen on screen. From that moment on I wanted to make films. And the first thing you have to do when you want to make a film is . . . get someone to write it. So I started writing films for the fun of it, making them with 8 and 16 mm cameras and a bunch of friends. I used to charge them money to be in my films. That's how I financed the pictures. I wish I could use that concept now. I came out of college with a degree in English and history, and moved back to Los Angeles with only one career in mind, writing movies. My background up to that point really consisted of trying to grow up, graduate from school, and not get anyone pregnant. I had a job like everyone else. I sold paint, was a truck driver, and an insurance claims adjuster. I started making a living at writing three years after I started.

Andrew W. Marlowe (*Castle, End of Days, Hollow Man, Air Force One*)

When I was a kid, my parents had something called "Movie Night," where they'd invite all their friends over, so I'd listen to all these academics discuss all these great films. I think this is when I first got the bug. I've always loved stories and storytelling. I was a member of the

Star Wars generation. I must have seen it close to forty times by now. It really opened my eyes to how movies could transport you to completely different places, and I think that at that age when you have a sense of wonder, you can get a sense of "I want to do the same for someone else."

From then, I took the normal circuitous route: I had a liberal arts education; I was an English major with a philosophy minor at Columbia. I had a media internship my senior year and became a production assistant on low-budget films and commercials. Then I got a job at a literary agency in New York, where I was reading the clients' scripts. Eventually, I applied to USC screenwriting program. My thesis script at USC won the Nicholl Fellowship at the Academy. From that came a couple of jobs and a lot of almost-getting-the-job, and because my thesis script was a small coming-of-age, I was in the small-coming-of-age pitching hell. So I decided to do something more exciting: I wrote an action spec that sold for quite a bit of money, and then I sold *Air Force One* on the pitch.

Bill Marsilii (*The Wind in the Willows, Déjà Vu*)

After marketing my first spec for a while, I ended up getting offers for representation from several agents, many of which came through referrals from an MGM executive who liked my work. But because I never expected to have all these options, I didn't know how to go about making the best choice. So I went to a screenwriter's forum online, where there was this professional screenwriter who had also broken in with a spec and who was really cool about answering people's questions. This was Terry Rossio. He asked to read my script, which he liked, and because he and his writing partner Ted Elliott were also producers, he asked if there were any other projects I was interested in. There was a children's Christmas book I'd found years earlier that I'd always thought would make a great idea for a comedy. Terry agreed, and we ended up pursuing the rights and pitching it to studio executives. TriStar said yes, and that's how I broke in.

Aline Brosh McKenna (*A Season in Central Park, The Ivy Chronicles, I Don't Know How She Does It, We Bought a Zoo, Morning Glory, 27 Dresses, The Devil Wears Prada, Laws of Attraction, Three to Tango*)

I took a class in my last year of college that was about screwball comedies, and I kind of fell in love with those movies. A year later,

I took a summer extension class at NYU, to see if I'd like it and if I was any good at it. We had to write a script in six weeks, and then I rewrote the script with the help of the teacher and a lot of my friends and that was the script that got me an agent and brought me to Los Angeles.

Scott Rosenberg (*Kangaroo Jack, Highway, Gone in 60 Seconds, High Fidelity, Disturbing Behavior, Con Air, Beautiful Girls, Things to Do in Denver When You're Dead, Air Time*)

I grew up in Boston and always wrote, even from a young age. I went to Boston University's School of Communications with a creative writing minor, where I managed to get into the graduate creative writing program. Upon graduation, I had no idea what I was going to do with my life, but the girl I was going out with moved to California, so I followed her. And when you're a writer in Los Angeles, you eventually discover this thing called a screenplay. Everyone I met was writing one, and I always loved the movies, so I started writing them. And everyone tells you to read *Chinatown* and *Lethal Weapon*, so I read the classic scripts and I just wrote.

I was always writing, probably four or five scripts a year in my lean years while doing every shitty job, like driving a truck, selling stuff door to door, working as a production assistant for Dick Clark, which was one of those eighteen-hour-a-day things, so I decided to apply to film school. While I was at UCLA, I placed third in the Samuel Goldwyn Awards, and that's how I got my first agent.

Terry Rossio (*Pirates of the Caribbean: On Stranger Tides, Pirates of the Caribbean: At World's End, Déjà Vu, Pirates of the Caribbean: Dead Man's Chest, Pirates of the Caribbean: The Curse of the Black Pearl, Shrek, The Road to Eldorado, The Mask of Zorro, Small Soldiers, The Puppet Masters, Aladdin, Little Monsters*)

I think stories about how people break into the business are by their nature misleading. In our case, it happened with a query letter to a production company, followed by—a year later—a meeting where we pitched a project to those producers that they liked, which we then wrote on spec, and they helped set up at MGM. I had identified the production company through a screenwriting newsletter. So that was the path that worked, but that doesn't mean the other paths we tried weren't valid. You never know the successful path until after the fact, so you have to try every path, all the time. Contests, seminars, shooting a micro-budget film, query letters, spec scripts, doing standup, learning animation, meeting people on message boards, mailing scripts to agents, stealing letterhead from agents and mailing scripts to studios, making a short film—any of those paths might turn out to be valid. You can't fire a single pellet out of a shotgun, even if only one pellet hits the mark.

Eric Roth (*Extremely Loud and Incredibly Close, The Curious Case of Benjamin Button, Lucky You, The Good Shepherd, Munich, Ali, The Insider, The Horse Whisperer, The Postman, Forrest Gump, Mr. Jones, Memories of Me, Suspect*)

I grew up in New York, attended Columbia University's film program, and did some graduate work at UCLA. I had some ideas of maybe becoming a director, but I was uncomfortable with that. I always loved movies, but I don't know what specifically made me want to become a screenwriter. I was well versed in film, a certifiable film nut. My dad was a publicist and a producer, my mom was a story editor, so I grew up in film. I just found myself writing a screenplay and I won the Samuel Goldwyn award at UCLA. So that's how it happened: I wrote a script, it won an award, it got produced, which led me to another job and it all went up from there.

Michael Schiffer (*The Four Feathers, The Peacemaker, Crimson Tide, Lean on Me, Colors*)

I started writing prose when I was twenty-five. I went overseas to get out of the culture enough to be able to write about it, and traveled through Asia, hitchhiked, had no money, spent seven months on the road and then, when I came back from that experience about two years later, I really began to write full time, writing all kinds of things. I wanted to be a writer and started writing novels. I also wrote plays, but I couldn't get any support from the playwriting world. I felt I got more respect out of the publishing world because it took me more seriously as a fledgling writer and gave me more creative support. So I put all my energy into doing that, but it wasn't an accident that after hitting my limit as a novelist, I drove to Hollywood when I was thirty-five to become a screenwriter. Directing theater in college made me want to write the stories myself. I gave myself five years and worked really hard, writing fourteen specs before I got hired for *Colors*.

Tom Schulman (*Welcome to Mooseport; Holy Man; 8 Heads in a Duffel Bag; Medicine Man; What about Bob?; Dead Poets Society; Honey, I Shrunk the Kids; Second Sight*)

Before writing, I was in production. I guess I began as a grunt, working odd jobs. I started working for a company in Nashville that made commercials and industrials, and my first job was carrying lights and doing pretty much everything. Then I came to Los Angeles and went to USC Film School, with aspirations to be a filmmaker.

Ed Solomon (*Imagine That, The In-Laws, Levity, Charlie's Angels, What Planet Are You From?, Men in Black, Leaving Normal, Bill and Ted's Bogus Journey, Bill and Ted's Excellent Adventure*)

I came into screenwriting because it seemed like the next step. I was writing on *Laverne and Shirley* when I was twenty-one and a senior in college, then went on to *It's Garry Shandling's Show,* and when I was twenty-three, I wrote *Bill and Ted's Excellent Adventure.* I didn't get into it with much thought. In retrospect, I wish instead that I'd had an idea for a novel and truly worked hard at it and sold it. I'd much prefer earning a living as a novelist because the process is the same. You sit in a room all by yourself and try to make up the most interesting, original, and true thing that you can, except with screenwriting the product gets chopped up and changed so much that the creative satisfaction is minimal.

Robin Swicord (*The Jane Austen Book Club, Memoirs of a Geisha, Practical Magic, Matilda, The Perez Family, Little Women, The Red Coat, Shag: The Movie*)

I've always wanted to be a writer from the time I first started to read. Though I did all kinds of writing, I didn't think about screenwriting because I didn't completely understand that movies were written. I began writing plays first, but by the time I was twenty-one, all I wanted to do was make films. I had worked as a photographer in college and had an understanding about the framing and images, which didn't translate to the stage. Someone had seen a play of mine in New York and got in touch with me. She asked me if I was interested in writing for film, so I sent her part of a screenplay. She read it, liked it, told me to finish it and that she would sell it. And she did. After that, people were talking about me as a screenwriter, not a playwright.

• • •

These twenty-two highly successful screenwriters have agreed to be your mentors and generously share their thoughts on the traits, skills, and habits necessary for success as a screenwriter in today's film industry. Let's explore them, shall we?

PART 1

PASSION

The Urge to Screenwrite

Cats gotta scratch. Dogs gotta bite.
I gotta write.

—JAMES ELLROY

CHAPTER 1

PORTRAIT OF A SCREENWRITER

1. Be Creative and Original

*The real voyage of discovery consists not in seeking
new landscapes, but in having new eyes.*
—MARCEL PROUST

Creativity is an essential skill for the professional writer, especially in screenwriting. Too many aspiring writers don't understand its importance. Ideas are king in Hollywood. Anyone who has read hundreds of scripts and listened to thousands of pitches could tell you that most of them are derivative of other movies, with familiar characters, uninteresting ideas, and clichéd plot twists. Beginners tend to develop the easiest idea that comes to mind, rather than working hard to generate original ones.

Tony Gilroy: Having a great imagination is 98 percent of the work. Originality *is* the job. It's what you do. Craft is craft, but it's imagination that puts you on the map. I'd rather work with someone who's imaginative with no idea what he's doing than an experienced writer with a limited imagination.

Derek Haas: You have to be creative and original or you won't get hired again. Even on sequels, assignments, or remakes, you have to find that original, creative spark. You have to take whatever the project is and make it your own.

Michael Brandt: Derek and I spitball together. We get together and smoke a cigar, usually with our manager, and we talk out the scenes or characters. We'll constantly call each other on being derivative or common . . . and we challenge each other to be more original or clever. When we hit on an idea that feels unique, we know.

It's crucial to understand that to be successful inside the studio system, a script has to be centered around a big idea. A big idea doesn't necessarily mean an expensive one, for the record. Three documentary filmmakers going into the woods to see if the Blair Witch legend is real is a big idea, shot very inexpensively.

Laeta Kalogridis: Original ideas and creative approaches are the heart of successful writing and moviemaking, even within the framework of established franchises or recognizable "brands." You can't survive in the business unless you're bringing something original to the table. That said, you can't make anything if you can't collaborate and do it well.

Bill Marsilii: The funny thing about Hollywood is that they want you to be original just like some other hit movie. I can't tell you how many times I've been told, "We want something original and edgy, Tim Burton-esque." And I'd think, "Gee, Tim Burton has already done Tim Burton-esque!" But this is what you will deal with once you break in.

Before this, however, as you work on your spec, it's crucial to avoid "first draft theater," where it seems that what you're reading is literally the first thing that popped into the writer's head. They didn't bother to examine it, to make it better, or to find a more clever or original way of writing it. They just settled for the first thing they could think of.

One of the ways I ensure that I go beyond the cliché is to go through a process I call, "Doing the 20s." I'll be writing a particular moment, and I'll stop and force myself to list twenty different ways to do it, like twenty cool ways my two characters could meet, or twenty cool chase scenes. The further you get down the list, the better they'll start to get. If you make yourself write twenty ideas, not worrying about whether they're any good or not, often the ninth or tenth one will be golden because you didn't settle for the first thing that popped into your mind.

Tom Schulman: Imagination and originality are crucial traits everyone is looking for in a writer because if someone has already seen what you've written, chances are they'll be bored by it. So when you conceive your story, characters, and plot elements, the key question is, "Is this something I've seen before?" and if so, you need to find an original approach to the material.

2. Be a Natural Storyteller

> *We're only interested in one thing: Can you tell a story, Bart?*
> *Can you make us laugh, can you make us cry, can you*
> *make us wanna break out in joyous song?*
> —*BARTON FINK*, BY ETHAN COEN AND JOEL COEN

You may love stories, whether you experience them through films, TV shows, novels, short stories, commercials, jokes, or plays, but if you can tell a story in the best possible way, make someone laugh, cry, feel pity, tension, curiosity, surprise, relief, or even inspire them, if you're compelled to captivate an audience, and know deep down that the most important factor in a story is its visceral effect on the audience, you may be a natural storyteller.

Robin Swicord: Writers have the sort of mind that puts together narrative in a way that has a beginning, middle, and end. They notice cause and effect—that because this thing happened, that other thing is happening. These are the kinds of traits that come together into a mind that makes drama. People who don't have that natural bend for it have a very hard time really understanding what it is writers do. There's nothing more humbling for people who say, "I've always wanted to be a writer" than to actually try to create an alternate reality, only to find out it's really hard to play God.

3. Be Comfortable with Solitude

> *Writing is a lonely life, but the only life worth living.*
> —GUSTAVE FLAUBERT

Writing is a lonely business. As a writer once said, "It's like volunteering for solitary confinement without knowing the length of your stay." Writers must spend a lot of time alone, but because they tend to be introverted by nature, they find more psychological comfort in a book or in writing than in social interactions.

This is not to say that if you're not comfortable with your solitude, you won't be able to write. One of the many surprises in chatting with our mentors is that many of them are actually extroverts who force solitude on themselves in order to do the job.

Ron Bass: I really prefer to write alone. Generally, when I have staff meetings, we talk about story and criticism, but I don't like to write with somebody else sitting there, because I'll talk out loud and I'll pace around. I can be physically active when I write. I usually sit but I also have standing desks wherever I go so I can write standing up, which enables me to pace around and charge back and forth, move my arms. It's a physical process, not just an intellectual one. I cross things out and I write bigger or darker depending on the emotion. If I'm in the park, I'll pace around. I must look really peculiar to people, so I try to find a place when I'm relatively alone, and certainly where I won't hear another human voice.

Leslie Dixon: In order to do the job really well, you must spend prolonged periods of time in total isolation. I loved it for the first few years where I had total control of my time without anybody telling me what to do. But I still haven't figured out how to strike a balance between spending enough time by myself to produce a better grade of work versus not becoming a hermit.

Tom Schulman: You need to create solitude so that you can hear the voices, and you need a willingness to live in the world of the story for long periods of time, forcing yourself into the world of the characters so that you can believe they exist. Many spouses of writers understandably complain that we're not living in the present.

Robin Swicord: A friend once gave me and fellow writers a personality test, and we all turned out to be introverts, which I don't think is a coincidence. Something like 20 percent of the general population is introverted, but I think most writers probably fall into that category. They feel very comfortable with solitude. They're probably better in one-on-one situations rather than dealing with lots of people. I know that when I'm in a room full of people, I tend to fall back as an observer.

4. Be a Natural Observer

Everything has beauty but not everyone sees it.
—CONFUCIUS

In order to describe, you need to observe. Most of us go through life only half seeing what goes on around us. We have too much going on to bother with observing details in life and in human nature. As a result, novice writers tend to reference what they've just seen on television and at the movies, rather than draw from what they've observed in the real world.

Successful screenwriters develop the habit of observing others, which gives them an ear for the way people talk and an eye for the way they behave. They're aware of the minutest details of the world around them, silently making notes on everything, and seeing things vividly and selectively. Whether in coffee shops, airports, or restaurants, they cannot resist eavesdropping on a conversation or people watching. In short, they pay attention.

Gerald DiPego: Beginners don't do enough observing or enough listening when they're out and about in the world, on buses, or in restaurants. Often, when I read a beginner's script, I find that the writer is not referencing life but rather what I see in movies and television.

Eric Roth: Everything is writing-related, you live with it twenty-four hours a day, so when you're out in the world, you're an observer of what people do and details of what's around you. Unconsciously, you try to save them and hopefully use them at a later time.

Robin Swicord: Writers have the particular makeup of a person who looks at the world, observes human behavior, and finds themselves amused, intrigued, or emotionally moved by watching people.

5. Be Collaborative

Your mind is like a parachute. It only works when it's open.
—ANONYMOUS

In no other form of writing is collaboration as important as in screen-writing. It's so engrained in the way scripts become movies that without this attitude, no screenwriter, unless he's a genius, can become success-ful. Once you receive interest from a producer to turn your screenplay into a movie, you will have to collaborate with development executives, directors, and actors. If you're difficult to work with, no one will want to be around you and you will develop a negative reputation that will hinder your screenwriting career. Collaboration is crucial.

Gerald DiPego: It's a whole skill you have to develop apart from writing. Call it compromise, negotiation, or debate. You spend a lot of time in development, trying to do your best to explain and defend the material against harmful ideas, but at the same time you have to stay open to the good ideas. Some people shut down and say, "The hell with them! They're all stupid." That's not going to work. Then again, you can't sit there like a stenographer and accommodate them because that will kill the material.

Derek Haas: You have to be willing to collaborate. Screenwriting doesn't end with "fade out." You have to be willing to work with pro-ducers, studio execs, directors, actors, cinematographers, stunt coordi-nators. If you think you're just going to type the words and the movie is going to reflect exactly what you wrote the first time, you're in the wrong business.

Michael Brandt: If you have a partner, it makes it much easier to collaborate. We're constantly rewriting each other. Our one rule is: just make it better.

Aline Brosh McKenna: One of the reasons I picked screenwriting as a career is that it's collaborative. So when I think of a new project, I also think about who my collaborators might be. And I usually have at least one primary collaborator on every project, whether it's a producer or director attached to the project, someone who can see the same movie I'm seeing, who has the same sensibilities about the project, who I can shoot small questions to or have conversations with to get me over the rough patches. That's enormously helpful. The more people you have, the better the experience.

Terry Rossio: I love collaborating with writing partners. It takes a team to make a film, so why not start with a team? That one decision naturally builds in a dozen key safeguards. You're less likely to work on a project that is of limited interest. You're less likely to procrastinate. You're less likely to work on something that has already been done. You're less likely to miss a key story problem. When working on a story together, neither person will have the answer to the problem alone, but somehow together you arrive at the answer. One plus one can equal three. One downside, though, is that the work takes about twice as long. It takes time and energy to reach consensus.

CHAPTER 2

DESIRE

6. Have a Driving Reason to Write

You have to have a dream so you can get up in the morning.
—BILLY WILDER

All of the successful screenwriters interviewed here have been writing for many years. They didn't get where they are today without having a driving and passionate desire to write. They may have other reasons why they write, but unlike many aspiring writers, not one of them only wishes to write a screenplay that will sell for a million dollars in order to have the freedom to do whatever else they really want to do.

Whether it's their primary way of expressing themselves, an outlet for their fantasies, or a desire to entertain people, real writers don't get satisfaction out of doing anything else. They love writing for its own sake. They love movies and they love to tell stories to a mass audience.

Ron Bass: There's only one reason to become a screenwriter, or a writer of anything, and that is you can't avoid it. It's what you love to do. It's who you are. I write because there's no way I couldn't write. I was writing stories when I was six years old because I loved to do it and tell stories in my own way. I wrote a novel when I was teenager, then I became a lawyer to support my family and was away from writing prose for sixteen years. And I really missed it. So I went back to it and didn't tell anyone that I was doing it. The second I started again, I just said to myself, "Why on earth did I take so long to come back to this?" There's absolutely nothing else in life that makes me feel the way that writing does.

Gerald DiPego: For me, writing borders on an obsession. It's almost like I don't have a choice, like breathing. While you can certainly rack yourself with doubt, there is a persistence about it where it isn't this sense of "should I do this or not?" but more "I can't help this, I love it, I need to do it."

Leslie Dixon: I was one of those little girls whose English teacher always told her she should be a writer. I had a dreamy identity that I was going be a writer since I was eight years old. I wanted to find some form of writing where I didn't have to work a crummy job and write at night, and since I was obsessed with movies, it seemed like the logical marriage of passion and commerce.

Akiva Goldsman: I couldn't think of a more perfect job for me. The act of writing is itself wildly solitary, but the act of making a movie is very social, so this is the perfect alternation: the solitude of writing and the community of building and making movies.

Nicholas Kazan: I started to write because I heard a line of dialogue and wrote it down, then I heard another one and eventually I wrote a play. Without knowing anything about the play when I sat down, I wrote this forty-minute play simply by transcribing these lines of dialogue. And the experience of having this entire dramatic work delivered to me by my unconscious was such a riveting and narcotic effect that I was hooked.

Jim Kouf: I write because I enjoy writing and I love movies. But the most important reason I write is because someone else likes what I write and is willing to pay me for it. Otherwise, I'd rather go fishing.

Tom Schulman: I've been doing it for so long now that it has become a habit. It's like when I haven't walked in the morning, I'm not in a very good mood. I just can't get away from it. I tried writing a novel, but unfortunately, every scene was two-and-a-half pages long. After a few chapters I thought, "Who am I kidding?" It requires the kind of patience that I just don't have. I don't even know if there are any bad reasons to become a screenwriter. Reasons and motivations are usually a cover for something else. Paddy Chayefsky once said that becoming a great lover was a good reason for writing screenplays, but you'd better have something else on your mind when you sit down at the typewriter.

Ed Solomon: I love a good movie just as I love a good book, but I don't love movies in general. I write because I enjoy sitting in the room making stuff up. I like thinking about dialogue and images and characters, which is fun and interesting, but putting it all together so that it becomes an interesting story is really hard for me.

Robin Swicord: I can't criticize anyone's dreams for wanting to become a screenwriter. Any reason is valid as long as it motivates you and you love to write. It's very difficult to make a living just writing, so every aspiring writer works two jobs. You have your day job, which helps you have a place to live and food to eat, and then you have your writing job, which takes place away from the rest of the world with very little support. Anyone who can do this for any length of time and is able to sell their work as a writer, no matter what it is, needs to be congratulated. So whether they want to be a screenwriter to be part of a microscopic minority of writers who actually make a living at it or whether they wake up in the morning with movies in their head and just have to write them down, whatever their reasons, they're perfectly valid.

CHAPTER 3

BELIEF

7. Believe You're Talented Enough

Having talent is like having blue eyes.
You don't admire a man for the color of his eyes.
I admire a man for what he does with his talent.

—ANTHONY QUINN

To do anything successfully, after the initial desire, you must believe it can be done. Strong belief is the driving force behind all art that was once visualized before becoming a reality. In Hollywood, it's not enough to have an "I think I can do it" attitude. It has to be "I *know* I can do it!" We are all blessed with talent. It's just a matter of noticing it and, more importantly, developing it. Anything is possible if you believe it. As Henry Ford once said, "Whether you think you can or whether you think you can't, you're right."

Michael Brandt: If you practice enough, you start developing a trust in your own abilities as you see the response you get. When we wrote that first script, it seems like everyone who read it wanted to help us. It kept getting passed up and up and up. That's when I first started thinking maybe we're good at this. Turns out that generally the stuff we liked was also good. Or at least we sold it that way.

Laeta Kalogridis: Even the best writers think they're terrible on bad days (or, you know, every day). Every aspiring writer has to walk the tightrope between having enough confidence to believe they have talent and something worthwhile to say, and being able to recognize when their writing is not working. The market may respond to you, it may not; that's not really the measure of a writer. Writers write. Nothing stops them. However, that doesn't mean you'll get paid.

Jim Kouf: You never know if you have talent. You're testing yourself with every script, so I never assume I've solved any riddles. I just keep trying to write something well. I never called myself a writer until somebody else called me a writer, and paid me for it. I wrote a script that got some attention and people started hiring me to rewrite other scripts. But it wasn't until I kept getting hired and I started making a living at it that I believed I was doing something right.

Eric Roth: Winning a contest helped validate me. It got me an agent but I've always had a real sense that I had a good visual imagination. I've always had the arrogance or confidence that I could write good characters. That's about it. I went through a learning process just like anyone else.

Michael Schiffer: The first thing any writer has to ask himself is, "How do I know I have talent?" The answer is, you don't know. When I first started out, I'd cook dinner for my friends, and then make them listen to what I had written that day. If I wasn't a good cook, there's no way anyone would have stayed. I could see them sitting there with such pity in their eyes, probably thinking this was just terrible and that I was just nuts.

Ed Solomon: Once in a while, you have an inkling that you may have a bit of talent when you make a little private connection by yourself in a room, a little scene that works or a great idea that surprises you. But the majority of the time, you're just slugging it out, confused, unable to see the forest from the trees, and doubting yourself, wondering if what you're saying has any value, or if you have the ability to make it work. Then when you finish something, and you think it's the greatest thing that's ever been written—three days later you feel it's an utter waste of ink and paper, and you wonder how you'll ever write anything again. I don't know how you overcome that. I just keep doing it because no one has offered me a better job yet.

CHAPTER 4

PASSION

8. Be a Voracious Reader

*Reading makes me want to write, and writing makes me
want to read. And both reading and writing make me joy to
be part of the great human adventure we call life.*
—KATHERINE PATERSON

Most writers grow up reading compulsively, feeding their minds with
great stories and planting the seed for future inspiration to write their
own. Good writers are good readers. Reading teaches the writer about
good storytelling the way watching an operation teaches a medical
student about surgery.

When our mentors are not writing or out socially they spend most
of their free time reading. They have a passion for the printed word,
whether it's fiction, nonfiction, or screenplays.

Terry Rossio: It's certainly best to have a breadth of knowledge of
as many genres as possible, across all media, including plays, television, novels, short stories, graphic novels, comic books, nonfiction
stories, comic strips, films, documentaries, pretty much anything.
That's the standard answer, and it's not wrong. But I hold an odd
belief. I think it's best to have an extreme depth of knowledge regarding a few select, favorite works, rather than a passing knowledge of
many works. Better to know every detail of how a few stories are constructed and how they function. As such, I find myself re-reading my
favorite top thirty books or so, more than being a "voracious" reader.

Michael Schiffer: Though I'm usually burnt out on words by the end of most days, I try to read a little bit before going to bed, and I read voraciously on vacation. I love to put my writing down and devour books.

Tom Schulman: Essentially, if nothing goes in, nothing comes out. What we do as writers, even though we deal in images, is use words. And the way we become literate is through reading.

9. Be Passionate about the Craft

If you don't love it without the money,
you won't love it with the money.
—TODD SILER

"Passion" is the most overused word in Hollywood, and for good reason. It's that critical quality that separates those who achieve their goal from those who simply dream about it. Every successful person has a passion for life, for their work, and for excellence. Our mentors are no exception. They're passionate about the craft of storytelling, the process and the work, which is far from a common trait among many aspiring writers. When would-be writers say, "I just can't find the time to write," this is a clue they're not serious about becoming screenwriters. When you're passionate about something, you're dying to do it as often as you can.

Michael Brandt: It really is a great gig. We get to work out of our houses, get to set our own schedules, and get to pick what time of day we feel like working. There are always deadlines and pressures but it's not like I'm putting on a suit and going into an office every day. And every now and then, I get to go sit in a darkened theater with an audience of ticket-buyers and watch something I wrote up on the big screen. There's no feeling like it.

Gerald DiPego: You've got to love storytelling and be a really good audience for film. I loved film long before I started writing it. I love its magic and how it takes me away. That's what made me want to be a writer. I wanted to be a part of that magic. No matter how many years you're in the business, it's always a thrill to see all that's been assembled around this fragile little thing called a story. Suddenly, people are hammering nails, building sets, and actors are walking around saying your lines.

Amy Holden Jones: I like purging my demons and fulfilling my fantasies. I like working out themes that matter to me. It's enormously satisfying to be able to work them out through characters I create and ultimately have a work that entertains a lot of people, especially kids. I also like the writing process, especially the refining stage after I'm done with the first draft.

Bill Marsilii: You must have a burning desire to tell stories on a visual canvas, to tell movies that will reach a wide audience and affect that audience emotionally. A screenplay exists to inspire a movie, one that will hopefully inspire an audience. If that desire is not front and center in what you do, then all you're left with is, "I'll write this because it's commercial and I think it could sell." Or, "Horror is hot right now, I think I'll write one of those," when they wouldn't be caught dead buying a ticket to see that genre. I write movies that I've always wanted to see.

Aline Brosh McKenna: What I like the most is having this thing you're creating that you feel you're in charge of, as if you're making this great lasagna and you get to figure out what the ingredients are and put it together and you're making something in the way it feels great to knit a sweater or refinish a table. The best days are when you went somewhere and you did some honest work. And there's some sweat on your brow and you came home.

Robin Swicord: I always loved creating a world. I love making up people and naming them, finding out who they are, what their great flaws are, and what they do and what they think is funny. And I also like that I can wear my pajamas to work.

10. Be Passionate about Movies

Let the beauty we love be what we do.

—RUMI

Just as a fiction writer learns to write by reading books, a screenwriter learns by watching movies and reading screenplays. Successful screenwriters love movies. They love their magic and how it takes them away in meaningful ways. It's this passion for movies, first and foremost, that gives writers an overwhelming desire to be part of that magic and tell stories for this most popular medium.

Nicholas Kazan: What distinguishes the people off the streets who want to be screenwriters from those who are successful at it is that successful screenwriters love movies, breathe movies, and have an overwhelming, almost narcotic desire to be part of the process.

Jim Kouf: When I was in elementary school, I used to rush home to watch movies. When I was in high school, I convinced a chemistry professor to let me make a film instead of writing a term paper. When I was in college, I thought I'd write plays because I fell in love with the theater. But when I moved back home I didn't have enough money to move to New York. It just so happened I lived in Burbank and the guy next door was a camera operator and the guy down the street was a makeup man and a friend of my parents worked at Universal, so I was able to get my hands on some screenplays to see what they looked like. Once I figured out the form, I was off and writing.

CHAPTER 5

COMMITMENT

11. Understand the Downside of Being a Screenwriter in Hollywood

You can take all the sincerity in Hollywood, place it in the navel of a fruit fly and still have room enough for three caraway seeds and a producer's heart.

—Fred Allen

Warning: This is an insightful look at the flip side to all the "first-time writer goes from waiter to hot writer" success stories you've read about in the trades. Consider this a public service announcement on the realities of the business and the reason why everyone says you need a thick skin to survive as a Hollywood screenwriter. Put every screenwriter on a bus out of town and see how quickly the industry comes to a halt: Producers have no movies to make, directors have no scripts to shoot, actors have no lines to speak, agents make no commissions, and so on with every job from production assistant to director of photography. No one has a job without a script, and yet screenwriting is the most disrespected element in the movie-making process. Why? Like it or not, film is still a medium driven by stars and directors. When a writer commits to a project, he goes home and writes it. When a star or director commits to a script, that project gets a green light for production.

Pay close attention. What follows is what awaits you as soon as you become a professional screenwriter.

Ron Bass: It's a very hard business. First, you're not the final decision-maker of what the final text will look like. This isn't true anywhere else. If you're a novelist, like I was, you can reject all your editor's notes and they'll still publish the book. If you're a playwright, no one is allowed to change a word without your approval. When you're a screenwriter—and I mean features, because if you're in television, you have some final decision power at the executive producer level— you won't have the final word, unless you're the director, and you'll go through losing things that are very precious to you and losing arguments that you think are essential to the integrity of the story.

Second, you're failing all the time as a screenwriter. The odds of anything getting liked are so small, and to get it made, they're even smaller. Even a wonderful script that everyone loves won't get made for all kinds of reasons. Even if it gets made, they may screw it up in making it or marketing it, and it may flop.

Third, you're always being criticized and rejected. And yet, if you don't remain vulnerable to that, you're hurting yourself. Those who can harden their hearts to it and say, "To hell with them, I don't care what they say, I know I'm right" can become arrogant and lack the openness [to accept] that maybe they don't have all the answers, maybe they're not doing such a great job and the criticism is correct.

Steven de Souza: For me, the problem is not the rejection, but the random factors of the industry. You can have a picture that's ready to go and the star pulls out. Suddenly, there's no movie. They weren't going to make the movie because they loved the script but because the *star* committed to it. You could have a movie ready to go and the management changes. The good news is that they don't want to make the movie. The bad news is that they want to *reinvent* the movie. You have a team, everything is in place, and one factor changes and suddenly the whole thing spins off in another direction. So half the time it's a horrible experience because the movie gets canceled and the other half it's a horrible experience because the movie gets made anyway, completely reinvented.

Gerald DiPego: Film necessarily comes out of a clash of opinions, unlike writing a novel, which is a solitary journey. In our film business, the writer's opinion does not carry equal weight with the other players. I love the writing, but after the writing comes the development. I don't know many writers who say they love development. That's where you're barraged by notes, and people give you changes. Some of them you respect as creative people, but others you wonder what are their qualifications, what makes them think they know how to make this scene better?

Tony Gilroy: The downside of this life is really poor. Not making it, or making it marginally, is really painful. Most of the people who try to do this are really smart. It appeals to them and you know why it appeals to them, so they're particularly prone to bitterness and disappointment, especially with all the things that can go wrong in this business, even when you're at the top of the game—like people ruining great ideas, or working for years on a passion piece only to discover someone else is doing the same story, or directors who don't know what they're doing rewriting you, or people not respecting what you do. Having an imagination that can take you almost all the way there means that it is also honed enough to turn against you and do all kinds of destructive things to you. It can be your worst enemy in a way.

Akiva Goldsman: There are certainly downsides to all things, but these are the choices we make. It's of course remarkably painful, without question, to get your ass kicked in reviews. I've gotten wonderful reviews and horrible ones, and the truth is, I've been the same writer from one picture to the next. Sometimes when a movie doesn't work, things get hung unfairly on one single individual when there's never a single individual who's responsible for a movie's success or failure. Sometimes I find that when writers get picked on in reviews, they get hit harder because they're hit by other writers. Ideally, if reviewers wanted to review a screenplay, they should read it and if they think it sucks, then they should say that.

Derek Haas: Sometimes things don't happen the way we expect them to . . . a good project dies or we get fired and replaced or the studio loses interest or for whatever reason, the stars don't line up on a script we poured our hearts and souls into. But we just compartmentalize it and move on to the next one.

Amy Holden Jones: Screenwriting is a terrible way to make a living and I always try to talk anyone out of it. Until you sit in a story meeting with the studio executives with no particular ability or actors who haven't even graduated from high school telling you exactly how to change your script, you haven't experienced what it's really like to be a screenwriter in Hollywood. Also, unlike novelists and playwrights, you don't own the copyright on your original material. It hurts when you sell a project you love and then management changes it, or they have no intention of making it and suddenly the project you really cared about will never see the light of day.

Laeta Kalogridis: The downside for me is the number of times you write something and it never becomes a film. Statistically most of your work will never be seen on screen. Unlike a novel or a poem, a screenplay is not a "terminal" form, [it's] more of a blueprint that many people will come together to use to create a film. You're part of a larger whole, which can be both wonderful—the collaboration—and frustrating. You can't make your work by yourself, which means of a necessity sometimes it won't get made at all.

Nicholas Kazan: In the theater, playwrights are revered and nothing can be changed without their permission. In film, directors rewrite you and actors change your lines without even realizing they're doing it. In that sense, it's a very frustrating profession. There are a million things that can go wrong with a movie. It can be miscast, a director can have the wrong tone, or a cinematographer can make the movie too beautiful or too ugly. And don't forget you can get fired. Even if you're successful, it still is incredibly painful. You write something you know would be a truly great film and it just gets destroyed. It may end up good or terrible, but it rarely is what it should have been, and you're the only one who knows this.

Jim Kouf: It's hard not to take it personally because here you are, the hero who slaved over these words, and as soon as you turn it in and everyone is happy with it, they couldn't care less what your thoughts are. It's a matter of giving up your child every time and letting somebody else raise it from that point.

Bill Marsilii: What I dislike is the utter casual disregard that so many people in the industry have for the writer's investment in the work, even people who should know better, who've been working with writers for decades. They so casually cast a script or the writer aside, without it even occurring to them that the writer might be affronted in some way. They love for you to be passionate about what you're writing, but after you've written it, you're expected to just shrug it off if they replace you. So it ends up feeling like you're being punished for caring.

It's painful when sometimes the reason they might choose someone else to rewrite you is because clearly you're so passionate about what you've written, that rather than ask you to change something and possibly be given a hard time about it, they'll just bring in somebody else who'll do whatever they want.

Scott Rosenberg: Screenwriting is so intensely collaborative that it's not as pure as writing a play or a novel. There are too many cooks in the kitchen. Even when you get to the point where the producer and the studio finally see eye to eye, the director comes in and tinkers with it, then the actors come in and tinker with it, and even after the movie is done, a test audience causes changes. The final product is never as pure as when you first sat down to write it.

Ed Solomon: What I dislike is everything that happens once you're done with a script.

Robin Swicord: I don't like that it's so cut off from the actual film-making process and that it's all about who has the money and who shouts the loudest.

12. Be Committed to a Career, Not Just One Screenplay

Concerning all acts of initiative and creation, there is one
elementary truth, the ignorance of which kills countless ideas
and splendid plans: That the moment one definitely commits
oneself, then Providence moves too. . . . Whatever you can do
or dream you can, begin it. Boldness has genius, power,
and magic in it. Begin it now.
—Johann Wolfgang von Goethe

If you're driven by the one-in-a-million chance of going from rags to riches overnight, nothing is stopping you from writing one spec script for money. But as you may already know, the odds are against you. To succeed, you need to think of screenwriting as a career, and to be committed to toughing it out for as long as it takes.

Laeta Kalogridis: People who are driven more by money than by love of the craft are at a disadvantage. Screenwriting is one of the few writing jobs where you can, if you hit the right combination of talent and luck, actually make a living. The odds are better than in, say, poetry, that a screenwriter can end up with disposable income, not to mention decent health insurance. But in my experience, the best writers are those who are driven by a love of what they do, who feel that they'll literally burst if they don't get things down on the page (and ultimately translated to screen). If your focus is solely on the idea that doing this job will make you rich, odds are against that outcome to begin with, and it can be corrosive to a person. Write because you love it, not because you want a Benz.

Andrew W. Marlowe: Any writer who is looking for the big payday so that they can buy their yacht and retire is not a professional writer. That's someone who's trying to win the lottery. The reality is that professional writers do project after project and bring a level of expertise to it that could tell all sorts of different stories. They never have just one big idea that defines their career; they have several that they can do very well. One idea does not define a career. Your career is the summation of dozens of ideas that you execute well. So as a professional writer, you're betting on your expertise, on your level of execution of that idea, that you can do it better than the other guy, or that your voice is distinctive enough that you'll be able to execute the idea in a unique way.

Terry Rossio: Our plan was to spend our time learning to write, continuing until we had a screenplay so good it was highly likely to sell, but if that took longer than ten years, give up.

13. Have Precise Goals, Not Just Wishes

All people dream; but not equally. Those who dream by night in the dusty recess of their minds wake in the day to find that it was vanity. But the dreamers of the day are the dangerous people, for they may act their dream with open eyes to make it possible.
—T. E. LAWRENCE

Look at all the habits so far. If they seem like too much work, you need to question whether your desire to write is a passion, a need, or simply just a wish. If you keep trying and failing to make the time to write, if your desire to write is not enough to keep you from doing more entertaining activities, then pursuing screenwriting as a career may not be for you.

But if you've committed to a writing career, and want to write for the sake of writing, you need to realize that wanting and doing are two different things. With distractions and obstacles everywhere, singleness of purpose and a compelling sense of mission are essential. A writing career is created. When you commit to it, you need a plan of action and you need to act on that plan.

Bill Marsilii: I did what all the books tell you to do and that no one actually does. I spent months just coming up with a good idea for a movie. And when I had one that really ignited me creatively, that I thought audiences would also want to see, and that people in the film industry might want to read, I outlined it vigorously and took it through two drafts on my own for a period of six months while working a day job, without telling anybody what it was about. I then gave the third draft to a number of trusted friends for their feedback, got their notes, did a fourth draft, and when I was confident that it was ready to show, I asked everybody I knew, if anybody *they* knew, *knew* anybody in the film industry who would be willing to give me some advice. That's three degrees of separation, and it resulted in about fourteen names. I figured people hate to be asked for favors but it's flattering to be asked for advice, so I didn't ask any of them to read my script. All I wanted was to meet with them for fifteen minutes and get to know them, learn their tastes in movies, and ask some smart questions (especially if there had ever been a passion project they wished they could sell their boss on), so that I wouldn't waste their time when I did submit a script to them. And most of the time, when they realized I wasn't crazy or overly pushy, and since it's their job to find new writers, they'd eventually ask me, "So what's this script you're working on?" And I'd answer, "Well, I can't really talk about it right now. I'm still working on it." And they'd be really curious about it, "No, go ahead, you can tell me." So I'd go into my pitch, and that opened a few doors.

14. Don't Let Self-Doubts Get in the Way

> *You have to be brave to take out that white sheet of paper and*
> *put on it words that could be evidence of your stupidity.*
>
> —Sol Saks

Ask any aspiring writer why he has yet to write his first script or why he hasn't finished the one he's been working on for years, and without hesitation he'll offer an endless string of excuses: "I don't have enough time," "I'm not good enough," "I have kids," "I can't afford the latest screenwriting software," or "I don't have an agent."

These excuses are often a front for self-doubt.

But success in any field can only come after you build your self-confidence. The good news is that confidence is developed. And in Hollywood, even a little bit goes a long way.

Gerald DiPego: It's very natural to doubt. By the time we're finished with the brainstorming process, there's a story in our head that really inspires us. But then the big doubt comes. Can I do it? Can I do it well enough? Can I transfer what's in my head to the page so that other people will feel what I'm feeling about this story? Can I make it sing? Can I do it justice? I think most of the fear comes at the very beginning, before we start writing. But after I bitch and moan to myself, this other voice comes in and says, "Will you just start?"

Leslie Dixon: All writers have doubts. But generally, as a person, I've always been comfortable and unafraid in most areas. I don't have this kind of desperation that most beginning writers have. It's just self-confidence without being arrogant. I think you need *more* self-confidence to say occasionally, "I don't think I can pull this off," and turn down the job if you know you're not the right writer for the project. It's just being honest that you don't always bat a thousand every time.

Akiva Goldsman: There's this wonderful notion, I think it's in *Three Kings*, where someone says, "Bravery is what happens afterwards." I've always believed that when you run across the battlefield with a flag in your hand, you're just trying to do desperately what the moment tells you to do. In the moment, you're just doing what's required. Afterward, you have the time to feel scared and proud and courageous. I'm constantly afraid of failing, of being found out and revealed to be a fraud, of writing badly and not being allowed to write again. Any creative person who doesn't feel some of that runs the risk of becoming complacent and then your writing suffers. You need a bit of self-doubt to propel you.

Derek Haas: You have to keep working at it. But at some point, you need outside validation. If you start getting outside, independent validation, then you can build on that.

Michael Brandt: But you'll never overcome those doubts. If you do, just read a screenwriting magazine and remind yourself how little you actually know.

Amy Holden Jones: Everyone has doubts. You overcome them with perspiration, by being critical of yourself, and trying harder, and when losing perspective, by pulling other people in, getting opinions, and acting on them.

Scott Rosenberg: In the beginning, I absolutely had doubts, and still do, but I wasn't crippled by them. I don't know why. I must have had this sort of misplaced arrogance about it. If I knew then what I know now, it may have been different.

Ed Solomon: Fears are the hardest part about writing, and the most debilitating is self-doubt. On the other hand, overconfidence and self-importance kill more creative souls than anything else, so you need to reach a balance between the two.

15. Educate Yourself

> *Learning by reading is like making love by mail.*
> —LUCIANO PAVAROTTI

Can screenwriting be taught? The proliferation of businesses and books catering to aspiring screenwriters shows that many believe it can. Despite some great writing workshops that help the writer learn the basics of the craft, thousands of formulaic spec scripts still flood an industry that abhors formulas (at least when it comes to buying spec scripts). That doesn't mean you can't learn valuable storytelling principles from attending a seminar or reading a screenwriting book. No one, however, can teach you the art of screenwriting because that's the unique magic only you can bring to a story. Seminars can be useful for interacting with fellow writers and inspiring you to write, but as you'll hear from our mentors, writing is self-taught.

In addition to watching movies and reading screenplays and books about screenwriting, a screenwriter needs to learn about life, people, the human mind, and emotions. Just as a musician learns by practice, working with and observing other musicians, or a painter by going to museums and studying the masters, you can learn by watching movies, observing other writers (what this book is about), reading screenplays, and, most importantly, writing them.

Ron Bass: When I was a freshman at Stanford, I took a literature course on the American novel taught by a famous novelist, a real writer, big guy, hard drinking, who'd talk about his days with Hemingway and Scott in Paris. I came up to him after class one day and said, "I really want to write fiction. What writing courses should I take?" He said, "Never, ever, ever take a writing course, never read a book about writing, never let anybody tell you how to write. Take literature courses, read, steal, turn everything to your interpretation. As soon as you take a writing course, it's the beginning of the end, because you establish somebody else as the authority for how you can write, and it can't be. Writing is an art; it comes individually out of you. Only you can express your art your way, it's an expression of who you are. I couldn't tell you how to write, Fitzgerald couldn't tell you, Faulkner couldn't tell you. They may tell you how *they* write and you may listen to them and some of that may help you."

My advice is to read screenplays, good ones and bad ones, so you can learn what you don't want to do, but more importantly, write a lot of stuff. You only learn to write by writing. Write every day. If it's a burden, you shouldn't be doing it.

Steven de Souza: [When I first started out] I got a couple of books that I still read to this day and highly recommend. One is *Vale's Technique of Screen and Television Writing*, which is still the best book on the craft I've ever read. The other is *The Art of Dramatic Writing* by Lajos Egri. The two complement each other because Egri's book is mainly about character while Vale's is more about structure and plot.

Most of all, you need to see classic movies. The problem with most movies made today is that they're imitations of last year's movies, which are imitations of the previous year's. Sometimes I mention a classic movie at a conference and no one in the room has ever heard of it. That's scary. It's like writing plays and never having read Shakespeare. You need to see all kinds of movies. Look at the silent ones, especially, because they had movies before they had dialogue. See how much they get across without dialogue. If you're depending only on dialogue to make your screenplays work, you're only working with half the ammunition that makes you a good writer. See a movie, then read its screenplay to see what was brought to the table by the actors and the director. Even a blockbuster can be a better learning tool than spending a weekend at a seminar.

Leslie Dixon: My mother was always dragging me to revival houses, so I was familiar with [Ernst] Lubitsch and Billy Wilder's work, for example. Watch a movie and read the script for it. You can learn more from that than any class. I tried reading a copy of Robert McKee's *Story* that someone lent me, and to me, it felt like trying to understand human beings by analyzing their DNA. It was so full of little charts and graphs and rules, it was mind-boggling. So much of what you have to do here is by instinct, and I think the best way to learn is by watching the movies *you* like and find out why you like them. Of course, all this is completely useless if you don't have some ability to begin with. That's a prerequisite.

Tony Gilroy: I learned by reading scripts and seeing movies, and becoming a freak about the craft. I was constantly looking at what scripts and films looked like.

Derek Haas: We took a screenwriting class in college and I read a ton of scripts as I was learning the craft. Yet, the most helpful thing was literally putting words on the page and finding a voice for us and trying it over and over. The more we wrote, the better we became.

Amy Holden Jones: I was lucky to be given a script to rewrite and direct, which was quite a learning experience. From this point on, I'd read the very best examples of the genres I was going to write. For instance, when I was writing *Love Letters*, I read *Kramer vs. Kramer*, *Ordinary People*, and other great dramas. If you read, analyze, and study them you begin to see patterns and techniques that work. Many beginners make the mistake of writing a particularly popular genre without even reading the classics in that genre. They also forget that the most important commercial factor in a movie is its visceral entertainment and that a script has to make you feel.

I also studied acting because Corman makes everyone working for him take acting classes. You learn the process an actor takes to create a character, how dialogue works or what makes a scene work, all valuable things to learn as a writer.

Laeta Kalogridis: I learned from watching movies, reading screenplays, and trying to analyze them to the best of my ability. What worked and what didn't for me? What narrative strategies did I find effective? When did I respond to characters, and when did I find them opaque or unbelievable?

Nicholas Kazan: I learned the craft by writing. Most seminars are social activities where aspiring writers can gain comfort from meeting other aspiring writers. What they teach is so far from the outside that it gives very little information to real writers. If you write five screenplays, the fifth one will be better than the first.

You'll refine your talent even without anyone reading them, even though it's better if others do read them, because you gain from what they don't understand or don't like. People's time would be much better spent trying to write screenplays than going to seminars. Make some labors of love. Write others quickly. Have the idea. Be inspired. Write it. Learn as you go. Watch movies. Read screenplays and write some more.

Andrew W. Marlowe: At Columbia, it was Aristotle's *Poetics*. Timeless lessons on dramatic construction. At USC, I was fortunate to have some outstanding teachers, like Frank Daniel, who was a master at deconstructing film. He taught great lessons on dramatic construction, sequence tension, how to keep your audience engaged. But I also furthered my education by watching movies critically. You could watch a movie for fun, and I can still get lost in one, but if you really want to learn the craft, you have to go back to your favorite films and look at them critically. Watch them deliberately, not as a fan, but as a form of deliberate study to see how they work.

Bill Marsilii: After graduating [from NYU], some friends and I formed a theatre company, which was an education in itself because as a "no budget" theater, we couldn't afford to pay royalties on anything, so we were writing our own plays; we couldn't pay our actors, so all the roles have to be good or they would quit; we couldn't afford advertising, so we depended on word-of-mouth, which meant the play had to be good. All we had was a title and a one-sentence listing in the Sunday *New York Times* to attract audiences, so we had to write "high concept" plays, where the title and the one sentence would make the audience go "no-name actors, never heard of this company, but this sounds good." Writing plays and seeing actors perform them, and seeing the audience respond, was a great education.

Aline Brosh McKenna: I read William Goldman's *Adventures in the Screen Trade*, which I love. I believe screenwriting is a discipline that requires practice. That's how I learned—by doing. Yes, there is some watching movies and reading screenplays, but there is some extrapolation that goes from watching movies to writing them that you can only get by practicing. The thing about being a screenwriter is that it's highly subject to practice.

I also learned from getting feedback, people around you telling you what works, what doesn't work, or how it affects an audience. And then going back and trying to fix what you worked on, learning to become an audience for myself and learning to go back and reread things, and see how close I got to what I set out to accomplish.

Scott Rosenberg: It's very difficult to teach someone how to write characters and dialogue. I believe that with the best screenwriters, it's a God-given talent. What you can learn, however, is structure. And you don't even have to go to film school to learn. You can pretty much get that out of a couple of books. The best course I ever took was taught by Frank Daniel, who used to be a dean at USC. He'd show you a film, then the next class, he'd show it again but with the volume on low and he'd talk over the movie, basically explaining how the whole thing worked structurally, what was planted here and how it was paying off there. He would do this on all kinds of movies, and it taught you everything you need to know about structure. Once you have structure, and if you can write character and dialogue, it's only a matter of coming up with good ideas. Another good thing about film school is that you have this shared experience with other writers and you don't feel so alone. You're also constantly getting feedback from other writers. Every week you have to turn in ten pages to your classmates to read and comment on. What was also great about UCLA is that you had to write six screenplays before they let you graduate. When you left school, you'd already be armed with a lot of material.

Terry Rossio: I learned the craft from my writing partner, Ted Elliott. I don't know where his abundance of ability and technique came from, though I can say he's the most well-read person I've ever met. When it comes to a writer improving his or her craft, I believe the best time spent would be watching plays or reading plays. Plays tend to showcase character, structure, and situation. And here's a wild thought: I also recommend studying songwriting. The hit song is a close relative to a hit movie, none closer. The issues a writer faces to write a hit song are exactly the issues a writer faces to write a hit movie.

Eric Roth: I learned by just being a film buff. I loved movies and knew the language. The rest you learn by writing. I think people also have to learn literature and plays. Dramatic rules will always apply. And a classical education is as important as anything because a well-rounded kind of knowledge is the best for any kind of writer.

Michael Schiffer: One thing I found helpful was taking some UCLA Extension classes in acting and directing. They gave you a sense of what a good scene is, what dialogue is all about, by seeing what actors do. It showed you how you're writing for people to say these words, and it gave you some experience in drama making. I highly recommend that beginning writers take an acting class. Be active in it, direct a scene with actors and see what animates the scene and what you can leave off the page. You can build muscles for writing good dialogue. I've never taken a screenwriting course so I can't really say anything about them. If you take the occasional seminar and come away with one great tip you didn't know before, that's a good thing. But I've come to believe you only learn on your own by doing it, by trying to tell stories that work. When you write twenty screenplays, you begin to internalize a sense of timing and movement of the story, structure, and dialogue. It's not somebody else's rules that matter, it's your own. If you do it by trial and error from the inside out, your work will find its own unique storytelling voice.

Ed Solomon: The most helpful any of the screenwriting books and seminars have been to me is once I've had eighteen years' experience writing. I think they're helpful at the very beginning . . . if you don't take them as holy writ. And they're interesting to look at after you've been writing a while and have had a chance to develop your own voice. But in most cases they can be dangerous. The book I'd recommend, which is about writing in general, is *Bird by Bird* by Anne Lamott.

Mostly, I learned by asking friends, but I'm still learning. The only difference is that now I'm learning more. The leaps I take are bigger. One of my biggest surprises was that every script needs to be written differently. What worked for the last one doesn't necessarily work for this one. Every time I start a new script, I really feel I'm relearning how to write. You just learn by writing, and living life. I try to understand this world and be a part of it.

Robin Swicord: I wasn't lucky enough to have a mentor, but finding someone who has the time and patience to sit with you can take years off the process. When I started to write seriously, I'd simply ask the help of people I'd meet whom I could see were smart, especially those who worked at the studios. It's very important to have someone from the outside who can read your work and be kind because you're risking everything when you're showing early baby work. At the same time, I'm not sure anyone can teach you how to write. All writing is self-taught.

What you look for when you search outside yourself is only another pair of eyes to help you see what you're not able to see because you're too close to the work. For me, it was watching movies, often seeing them a second time because I'm a sucker for narrative. When I see a movie I get sucked into the story so I have to see it again and really pay attention.

Sometimes, I tell people to watch movies on video with the sound off and watch what the editor has done, where the cuts happen, how information is conveyed visually, why a scene begins here and not earlier or later. The way humans learn is to absorb all that stuff, and that understanding of other work goes into the understanding that makes our own work.

16. Be Willing to Make Sacrifices

*You can achieve anything you want in life if you have the
courage to dream it, the intelligence to make a realistic plan,
and the will to see that plan through to the end.*
—SIDNEY A. FRIEDMAN

When you talk to aspiring writers, you realize most don't want to
write; they want to have written. They aspire to the rewards of writing,
like the finished screenplay that sells for a lot of money, not the hard
work that goes along with it. They believe that writing a movie is no
harder than watching one, that success can happen overnight if only
they had the right software or the right connections.

The reality is that writing a script is probably one of the hardest
things you'll ever do. Committing to a screenwriting career also means
sacrificing most of the things we take for granted—dating, getting married, having children, a steady income, health benefits, traveling. If
struggling and honing your craft seems more attractive to you, if you
give the craft every fiber of your being and think, eat, sleep, and breathe
screenwriting twenty-four hours a day, without a guarantee you'll ever
make it, you may be a real screenwriter, like Ron Bass, who works an
average of fourteen hours a day, seven days a week; Eric Roth, who likes
to wake up in the middle of the night, write for a few hours, take a nap
and start again in the morning; or Akiva Goldsman, who goes straight
from bed to his computer and writes nonstop for ten to twelve hours.

The rest of our panel, with a couple of exceptions, keep regular
hours, eight hours a day, five days a week, like any other job.

Akiva Goldsman: I was lucky early on, but the downside was that
my career became my life. Now I'm divorced, and I might not be had
my career not been as wonderful but as consuming as it was. This
business is so hard to get into that once you do, you never want to let
it go and the ability to regulate your participation doesn't come easily. I still don't have it. I'm still wildly engaged with the idea of making
movies and being part of them, and it's as tantalizing and delicious as
any experience. But with the good comes trading off. Sometimes, like
with anything in life, other good things fall by the wayside.

Jim Kouf: I was committed to making it in show business. I refused to date or do anything else but write. I was writing nights and weekends and I wasn't happy until I did it. I ate, slept, and thought of nothing but writing. The only thing that would have forced me to quit is if I couldn't make it after ten years.

Luckily, I started making a living at it after three years and I haven't been unemployed since then, except for a couple of writers' strikes. I didn't have a family when I started out and I don't recommend having one when first starting out because at the very beginning, show business will steal your life. You have to be totally committed to getting in, you have to live, eat, breathe it, meet people in it, and become friends with them.

Michael Schiffer: I wanted to be a writer and I was desperate. I was living on $3,000 a year. It was make it or die. That's a great motivation, not having any other way to live. I came to Hollywood with very little money and found odd jobs to support myself. I was willing to say I gave it my best shot. If it didn't work out, I was going to walk away from it at age forty. But the first part of that is to actually give it your best shot. None of us knows about our talent but we can address the hard work and the craft part.

17. Set a High Standard of Excellence

> *I've learned early on, that no one discriminates against excellence.*
>
> —Oprah Winfrey

Put simply, highly successful screenwriters are successful because they do the job better than anyone else. When starting out, our mentors took the necessary time to develop their craft. They knew what it took to make it and that they had to write more than one script to achieve the requisite craftsmanship to gain attention. Now, they're ruthless in their desire to do their best. They have to be—their livelihood and reputation depend on it. A few slipups into substandard levels and they know they'll be replaced by the latest hotshot young writer.

As a beginner, you need to know what this standard is and raise your work to meet it. Read great scripts and compare them to yours. You'll see the difference on the page and, hopefully, it will inspire you to raise the quality of your own work.

As Oscar-winner Michael Arndt (*Little Miss Sunshine, Toy Story 3*) once said, "After working ten years in the film business as an assistant and a script reader, I had read enough mediocre scripts that I was determined not to inflict another one on the world."

Michael Brandt: A lot of beginners see a crappy movie at the theater and say, "I can do better than that." You have to understand that your competition is not the crappy movie at the theater. Your competition is the thousands of great scripts that are trying to break through the clutter every year.

Leslie Dixon: As a screenwriter, I went through a horrific learning curve. My first script was basically sold on the idea. I continue constantly to feel my work is not good enough and try to improve it every day. To this day, I've never felt that my work pops out of the gate fully formed. So much of it is diligent and grinding application. It doesn't come easily to me.

Akiva Goldsman: Joel Schumacher taught me that if you just do your job well, you're doing better than 90 percent of the people doing it because so few people actually really do their job. He also taught me that there's room for error but no room for sloppiness, and this is really important to know because in the movie business, there are a lot of people relying on everything you do. If you take your work seriously from the get-go, you have a better chance of fitting into the business once you're in it.

Bill Marsilii: The concept is the most critical aspect of a screenplay, especially for someone trying to break in. You can be the most talented jockey in the world but if you sit on top of a mule, you'll never be able to race with professionals. I see too many beginners ignoring this point. They see a movie and then try to write one just like it. I don't need a new writer to come up with another buddy cop script. There are already plenty of pros who can do it and do it very well. But if you have an idea that nobody else is writing out there or has done before, even if it's not executed that well, Hollywood will buy it from you and throw twelve writers at it. And once you're in the door, you'll have a chance to write something else.

• • •

You've got passion, you've got desire, but have you mastered the habits that boost your creativity? Our mentors have. Let's find out how you can, too.

PART 2

CREATIVITY

Summoning the Muse

*O light supreme, raised so far above mortal thoughts,
lend again to my mind a little of your epiphany and give
my tongue such power that it may leave a single
sparkle of thy glory to future men . . .*
—DANTE, IN *THE DIVINE COMEDY*

CHAPTER 6

THE CREATIVE PROCESS

Feeding the Muse

In order to generate creative energy, you must first fuel the brain. . . .

18. Get Input as Often as Possible

In the midst of our daily lives, we must find the juice to nourish our creative souls.

—SARK

There's a computer term called GIGO, which stands for "garbage in, garbage out," meaning you only get out of the machine what you put into it. This applies to ideas as well. Because writers abound with natural curiosity, they tend to be information junkies. They are sponges for information, immersing themselves in the outside world and soaking up enough of it, not only to know what's been done so they can be different, but to fill their lives with enough raw material that will eventually spill out with their unique signature.

Steven de Souza: I'm a mad newspaper clipper. I have a wall completely devoted to filing cabinets, half of which are clippings, anything that gets my attention, like outrageous or clever crimes, incredibly stupid criminals, robberies, the latest technology, police techniques, military weapons. Technically, I research all the time even though I don't know if it'll pay off some day. I also love the Internet because of the amazing access you have to things. I spend about thirty minutes a day zipping through news websites, and I also have an assistant who finds me obscure things.

Amy Holden Jones: Reading the newspaper is a big source for me. True stories of things people have done and the way they actually behaved often surprises me.

Scott Rosenberg: You definitely try to watch a lot of movies. I prefer not to read scripts because I don't want to know what's out there. When I'm not socializing, most of my free time is spent reading. But more importantly, it's about getting out there and living a life that's not related to the movie business, which is very hard to do in Los Angeles. If you spend enough time here, you come to realize that all the people you surround yourself with are in the movie business, used to be in the movie business, or want to be in the movie business. Sure, it can be very seductive when you find yourself at a party and there's Brad Pitt and Tom Cruise, but at a certain point, you have to say to yourself, "Wait a minute, I'm supposed to tell stories that are universally recognized and that's tough to do when I'm drinking a beer with Tom Cruise." It's not reality.

Tom Schulman: More than watching movies, I read a lot of fiction, nonfiction, newspapers, magazines, or I browse the Internet. But fiction is the most important. For some reason, if I don't read fiction, I have difficulty writing.

Robin Swicord: As writers, we need a lot of cultural input just for the sake of keeping our own minds alive. We also need to make ourselves get out of our pajamas and go out into the world and do something that's just human contact with other lives. As a human being, all you really have to write from are your own experiences, your own mind, and your own perception of the things that inspire you. You have to be interested in a lot of things. Do some volunteer work. Be involved with the world. The writing is just one aspect of who you are as a person, but who you are as a person is what feeds that writing.

19. Don't Worry about Finding Ideas

The best way to have a great idea is to have lots of ideas.
—LINUS PAULING

Our mentors don't worry about finding ideas. For them, it's more like, "so many ideas, so little time," because their attitude is that ideas are everywhere. You just have to be open to them. If you're aware of what interests you, what sections you tend to browse in the bookstore, what TV shows you like to watch, what movies you can't wait to see, you will constantly be coming up with new ideas.

If not, go deeper: What lights you up? What fascinates you? What disturbs you? What frightens you? What disgusts you? What do you find attractive? What do you hate? What do you love? These questions should lead you to a subject worth writing about.

Ron Bass: Finding ideas has never meant that much to me. I've never felt very proud of that. I'm a storyteller. I'm not necessarily the person that gets the initial idea. They could come from anywhere—personal experience, people who work with me. Very often it comes from the buyers. They tell me their idea and then I'll write the story around it, like spinning the pearl around the grain of sand.

Akiva Goldsman: I don't spend any time hunting for ideas. I find that the world is full of ideas and you just have to be open. They come to you and the really good ideas are the ones that possess you and you ultimately end up using.

Scott Rosenberg: I have too many ideas and it's very frustrating because there's no way I could get to them all. I aspire to get to a place where I can hire young writers to write a first draft under my supervision.

Ed Solomon: I find that when you're open to ideas, they come, and when you search for them, they don't. The more you're open to the world around you and are thinking in that way, the more ideas come. It's absolutely true for me that writing breeds more writing and the more you are active in thinking and writing, the more ideas you get. A big part of it is pushing, nurturing, and fertilizing the ideas that come.

Robin Swicord: My problem is what am I going to do with all of them? I don't have enough time to write all the stories that come into my head. My mind is like Velcro. I don't look for them; they look for me.

Nurturing the Idea

Once you're blessed with the germ of an idea, you prepare by searching for raw materials that will become characters, plot, bits of dialogue, or situations. As you look at the big picture, ask questions and let your mind wander. . . .

20. Ask the Right Questions

> *The answer to any problem pre-exists. We need to ask the*
> *right question to reveal the answer.*
>
> —Jonas Salk

When it comes to storytelling, the most popular story starter is, "What if?" Asking the right questions often brings the right answers, like nails to a magnet. Most screenwriting books are filled with them: What is my story about? Who are my main characters? What do they want and what prevents them from getting it? Why do they want it? How far will they go to achieve it, and how far will someone go to stop them? Where and when is the story taking place? Two other, often overlooked questions are, "Is this unique and compelling enough to interest an audience?" and "Am I moved by this in any way?" Because if it doesn't move you, the writer, it definitely won't move an audience.

Ron Bass: Once I get the germ of the idea, there's a process I call "matrixing," which is everything that happens before I outline, a sort of gathering of ideas. I think about things in a deliberately disorganized way because I want to be free and open to anything. I gather everything in whatever way it strikes me. I go to the park and pace around and write out every idea that comes to me, whether it's about plot, structure, character, dialogue, theme, or tone. I'm writing everything like crazy for days or weeks.

Laeta Kalogridis: Usually, I'll find something—an image, a text, a song—that makes me think of something, and I'll start taking notes about the world, the characters that could inhabit it, the kind of story they'd live. Then I outline, usually at least forty pages, and then start writing. After I've written the draft, I show it to friends. They give me notes, and I rewrite. A number of times.

Nicholas Kazan: Often an idea starts with a feeling, or I see a character in the street and he does something interesting, and I start wondering why, and I just follow that wherever it goes. Frequently, it goes nowhere, but what happens is that by writing it down, an idea leads you to other ideas, and sometimes the ideas will fall together with other ideas and make a whole. I don't use cards or any structural paradigms. I just write notes and outlines, thoughts about characters, dialogue, and scenes, and I just try to play for as long as I possibly can. It's sort of an exploration of the world of the screenplay.

Aline Brosh McKenna: I always connect with characters. Like in art, I connect with portraits. That's how I think of screenwriting: connecting with portraits. So I always start with characters or relationships. Concepts that don't suggest specific characters don't inspire me. When I have an idea, it should suggest some people or it's not going to be the right idea. The characters should tell you what they need to have happen, what they need to say and do, and where they need to go.

Terry Rossio: The first issue, and most important, is whether the concept of the movie is intrinsically compelling. I like to feel with absolute certainty that the fundamental idea for the film is an exceptional premise, one that implies that a film must be made from it, without question. Next, I ponder why the concept is compelling, like examining a diamond from every angle under different lighting, against different backdrops. Yes, you know it's pretty, but what makes it so? And how does it achieve its beauty, and could it be enhanced even more? Once you discover several different ways a premise is compelling, you can attempt to know how best to present it. Would the 'interesting stuff' be better explored as comedy, a drama, a police procedural, a western? Even if you have a genre in mind that seems obvious, it's worth thinking about how the idea plays in other genres.

Right away I start to see key images. There is nearly always a series of filmic images naturally associated with every good film idea. As these images come—trailer moments—I try to think of ways to link them or group them, to write toward them and away from them; a plot starts to form. Next, I spend some time thinking about the all-important "second idea."

Since I fear working on something that isn't great or compelling from the start, I want to stack the deck in my favor by taking the first inspiration and going past it, add to it with a second inspiration. This is hard to describe because it could be "adding" or "merging" the first concept with another concept from another movie idea, or it could be coming up with some twist that derives from the original idea and pushes it further. I always keep thinking, "How can I push this more than what I already have?" Can I do the entire concept in the first thirty pages, and then go from there, and really blow the audience away? This is all fear-based—"Is it good enough? No, not yet. I can do more."

I don't go too far without starting to think about the main character relationships in the film. Not the main character, or characters, their histories and such. That's not so important. To me, the relationship between characters is what needs to be defined, those are the moments audiences desire, and the characters can be adjusted to make the main relationship or relationships more interesting. This leads to thinking about what kind of character, and character situation, is best to mine the concept, or take best advantage of the story arena.

I always try to think of ways to push the characters into extremes, because this is my personal weak point, and I worry that my characters are too timid or bland, too much a reflection of my actual self or the self I wish to present to the world, and not enough a reflection of my hidden self—my fears, experiences, dreams, wishful thinking, intuition, hangups and psychosis; or that they're not compelling or unique enough.

I try to think of situations, or evolving situations. My goal is from page one to present whatever the story is in only a series of "characters in situations" where the information and issues appear as a side effect of people dealing with immediate problems, with no relief. I ask myself if I've made the mistake of making the secondary characters more interesting than the leads.

Early in the process, I want to focus on the ending. Nothing else matters, no project will begin or get anywhere or make any progress until the ending is known. If there is no satisfying ending, or at least the glimmer of one, the idea will sit on the shelf. Good endings are hard. But once you have one, everything else derives from the ending, because it's all, in a sense, setting up that final twist, emotion, feeling, thematic statement, rush of excitement, chill, brilliant payoff, or sublime wisdom.

I always ask what the tone is. This takes me back to genre. Are there genre conventions that can be mixed, or used to advantage? Is this really a *Romeo and Juliet* story, hiding in disguise? Is it really *The Count of Monte Cristo*? Is it *The Guns of Navarone*? *Once Upon a Time in the West*? Is it an innocent on the run, like *North by Northwest*? Is it a combination of story patterns, or is it something that's not been done before? If so, how do I see the pattern in my head?

What's the title? If the project doesn't call to mind a cool title, then I start to suspect it's not a good project, or I'm not ready to write it yet. Has a theme emerged yet? It's almost impossible to have the makings of a story without a theme implied. But then I ask if the theme is trite, or is the opposite of the obvious theme more interesting? Is there an entirely different theme that's actually better, more sublime, more compelling? I also explore whether all aspects of the theme, or central question of the screenplay, can find form in the story—perhaps characters or relationships can be invented by assigning them different aspects of the thematic argument. Then I ask, "What is a compelling opening image?"

At some point, after having a few characters, scenes, and images in mind, I wonder what the point of view is. It usually starts off flying all over the place to explore the story, but is there some way to *limit* the point of view that would actually enhance the telling of the story, like "What if we revealed stuff from *this* character instead, how does that change the emphasis, how does that change the unfolding narrative from the audience's point of view?"

I double check if the setting is right. What if I changed the gender of my lead, would it matter? What if I opened at the end instead of the beginning? Would the whole thing be better if the leads were ten years old? These are just routine questions used to double-check the whole creative process, shake things up, and make sure I'm fully exploring all options.

I might ask if this is really best suited as a screenplay—is it really a novel, a short story, a play, a comic book, or a television series just masquerading as a feature screenplay? I double-check if this is castable, if the budget is under control, if it's something a director might like to make, if actors will want to be in these roles, because I want the thing to get made! I also wonder if I've fulfilled, and also exceeded, the genre. If it's a horror film, is it actually scary? If it's a romance, is it actually romantic? What are the reference films the audience will bring to this? I wonder if this requires a character as villain or is it not that type of film. Is the conflict not imbedded in one person? What if there were two villains? What if the villain turned out to be the hero? What if we told the story from the point of view of the villain?

At some point, the process of generalizing breaks down and I have enough answers to get into specific story problem solving. I start to generate ongoing patterns—character relationships, setting up reversals, building surprises. I play around a lot with the "lines of force," which is just tracking each character through the story, understanding the audience will expect each character to continue toward the path of what they want, unless events conspire for their wants to change. All actions are a result of intent, and intent comes from desire. Character desires have to be designed so that the plot occurs as a by-product.

I always ask what's cool. What's a cool sequence, character, line of dialogue, setting, sequence, relationship, demise, fight sequence, visual, or cool opening image? I repeat this whole process several times, as needed, until in an excruciatingly slow process, each solution asserts itself and declares itself "good." And finally, when everything is good or I run out of time, I start writing the screenplay.

Eric Roth: I let the idea germinate for a bit. I'm usually interested in the people and the theme associated with the germ of the idea. So I first need to know what it's about, the theme, because usually the story and characters should reflect that theme. Then I try to get very secure with what my opening and ending will be. The opening and the ending never change, and the middle is a big blur.

Robin Swicord: This is one of my favorite parts of the creative process. It's like writing the genetic code of the seed that will grow up to become a screenplay. I spend a lot of time thinking and making notes and playing out little scenarios in my mind to figure out the central theme of the story and things about the characters. I imagine ways to make it as visual as possible, how scenes will push other scenes, or whose voice will be heard above the crowd. It's a very long process.

21. Research

The mind is not a vessel to be filled but a fire to be kindled.
—PLUTARCH

In this age of Google, Wikipedia, IMDb, and a million other sites on the Internet, information is not only ubiquitous but also fun and addictive. Whether you're searching for information about countries, cities, occupations, time periods, or that exact word to give your scene a ring of truth, it's often only a few clicks away. But be aware that researching can easily become a form of procrastination that can take more time than necessary and trap you from actually writing anything.

Steven de Souza: I do whatever research I need as late as possible because I don't like to interfere with the creative flow. So if I'm writing about a city I haven't been in, I'll look at a map or read an article about it, just enough to get through, and I'll check on the details later. I don't want to stop in the middle of an emotional scene and have to go to the library to get a travel guide to that city.

Leslie Dixon: Writers can get lost in research and use it as an excuse not to get on with the writing. Up until recently, I never did any research and faked absolutely everything. In the arena of comedy, it's more about giving the audience a good time. You really don't need to be factual and have the body of knowledge you would need if you were writing *The Insider*, for example. I know one writer who did six months of research and a lot of the momentum in her career was killed by staying out of the marketplace so long.

Bill Marsilii: I feel it's a productive form of procrastination because it often creates a certain amount of comfort in the world that you're writing in. I like to buy books and DVDs that are about the world I'm writing. Sometimes, I go to a key location. For *Déjà Vu*, I went to the Brookhaven National Lab on Long Island and toured its particle accelerator, which led to a couple of key plot points in the story. You never know what's going to be useful.

Terry Rossio: Film is a visual medium, so the best research is visual. We like to look at children's books, as those are designed to focus on the elements of a topic already in the public consciousness, the most iconic.

Michael Schiffer: I do some book research, but most often I go out with a tape recorder and spend as much time with people as they'll possibly give me. I like to talk to people who do the job I'm writing about. I spent six weeks in a bulletproof vest with cops and sheriffs for *Colors*. I've been on a nuclear submarine for *Crimson Tide*. It's the most fun part of my job.

Playing with the Idea

You transform and manipulate the resources you find by putting on your child's cap and letting your imagination roam free . . . .

22. Become a Child

> *Genius is childhood recovered at will.*
> —CHARLES BAUDELAIRE

Remember when you were a child? Filled with wonder, free to play, spontaneous, living in the moment—life was a creative adventure. Everything around you seemed interesting, magical, and exciting. You loved to experiment, take risks, explore without boundaries, and touch.

Think about the power of your imagination when you first discovered drawing, colored pencils, paper, or when you experimented with your first piece of clay. Or you played with dolls or action figures—make-believe, cops and robbers, imagining scenes and dramatic situations. Losing yourself in play brought you joy and excitement.

This is exactly what writers become when they're creating scenes and getting lost in them. Like children, they have a fondness for playacting and make-believe. At this stage of the creative process, they loosen up and get in touch with this same sense of wonder, curiosity, and risk. This is where they get to play and experience that joy of discovery, of being in the moment, and of taking chances and seeing where they lead.

Robin Swicord: In one corner of my office, I have dolls and childhood things because I feel the beginning of what we love and what we become happened when we were children. What I did as a child is the same as what I'm doing now, so having things from my childhood are like talismans that remind me of what I'm really doing, which is sitting on the floor with my legs out, and on the floor between my legs, I have dolls and paper and glue and scissors and I'm making costumes and naming characters and whispering dialogue and planning great stories and having adventures in my mind.

The only difference is that now I'm doing it for the pleasure of an audience. People sometimes forget to get in touch with that feeling. They don't give themselves permission to think of themselves as children playing. The most wonderful feeling is that of being at play as a child and it's our job as writers to let the child out and be creative. What is so amazing is that when we grow up we never have to stop playing. We have to be adults and be responsible, professional people. We have to turn our work in on time and be good collaborators, but at the most basic level, we get to go away from the rest of the world, shut the door and play.

23. Become Possessed by the Story

Creation is a drug I can't do without.
—Cecil B. DeMille

Whereas the habit of becoming a child is more concentrated in specific moments and scenes within a story, there's a point in the creative process where you become obsessed with the story as a whole—you're thinking about it all the time.

Amy Holden Jones: Sometimes I'll start with a scene or a mood and elaborate on it, let it take me where it takes me. But often what happens is that I'll write thirty pages and there's nowhere to go after that.

But from these thirty pages, I usually stumble on an interesting character, a scene, or a thought, and I go back to the other more secure process.

Nicholas Kazan: I like the feeling of being possessed by the story. Good screenwriters hear dialogue and see pictures. And while they have to devote enormous amounts of time to construction, they become possessed by their stories. By that I mean that they don't make up their stories. They don't say, "Gee, I wonder what's selling?" The good writers have an idea of what will happen in the scene and the characters speak to them. So rather than asking what the characters might say at a certain juncture, the writer watches the characters speak.

Bill Marsilii: For me, it's about spending months just coming up with the basic premise, the great idea. Far too often, writers will take the first idea that comes into their heads and start running with it, without bothering to think, "Is this really a great idea for a movie?" And if it isn't yet, is there something in it you can't stop thinking about, and could you turn *that* into a great idea for a movie?

Once I'm thrilled by the concept, I open up a Word file and start writing any cool thing I can think of—scenes, sequences, locations, even a single line of dialogue, even if I don't know where it'll end up. If you look at the idea as the "spark," then this process is akin to adding kindling to the fire. And if every cool idea brings to mind two other ideas, and you reach a point where there's this huge creative brushfire in your brain, and you find yourself writing page after page after page, then that's great. That's when I know I've really got something here. And if I start to wonder, "How can I possibly do justice to all these cool ideas in only 120 pages?" then that's fantastic. If you feel that this would be an "easy" story to write, if you're not scared by the daunting challenge of crafting something meaningful out of the idea, then chances are it's a crappy idea.

As soon as I start to see a narrative spine for the story, I start writing things on index cards, one idea per card, which I keep in a little recipe box, or bundled up together with a rubber band when they're in my pocket. In the early part of the process, I have no idea about the order of the cards. After a while, I start to get a sense of where things go, and I start rearranging the cards, which in a subconscious way makes me think about the structure. I reach a point where I start to see the movie in my mind without too many skips, and when I reach a critical mass, I go to the outlining process.

Scott Rosenberg: Once the idea occurs to me, I immediately people it and ask myself who are my characters. Then for about a month, I live with it for a while. I drive with it, I take it to dinner, it's the last thing I think about before I go to sleep and the first when I get up in the morning. I sort of let it percolate.

Simmering the Idea

At a certain point, you need to let your overworked mind rest. Walk away from the playground and turn it over to your subconscious, which will digest what you have for a while.

24. Be Aware of Your Muse's Favorite Activities

Make friends with your shower. If inspired to sing,
maybe the song has an idea in it for you.
—ALBERT EINSTEIN

Although they don't seem to do it consciously, writers put themselves into situations that foster creative thoughts and allow their subconscious to help out. Asked when they usually come up with bursts of original ideas, our mentors answered: While driving; showering; taking a relaxing bath; or performing any manual activity, such as shaving, putting on makeup, cooking, gardening, or exercising. They might be walking in nature, swimming, or jogging. It happens when they're reading, listening to music, sitting on the toilet, doodling at a boring meeting, and falling asleep or waking up—especially in the middle of the night. You'll notice most of these activities tend to free the mind to think, while their rhythms and routines put the body on automatic pilot. Put simply, these activities are just "disciplined inspiration." By making it a daily habit of just being aware of and prepared for these activities, you allow these heightened moments of inspiration to enter your consciousness on a regular basis.

Ron Bass: I get up very early. It used to be around three in the morning, now more like around four. But the "writing" starts before I get up. Right around the 3:15, 3:30, 3:45 of it all, I lie there thinking about the scene, I go there, and eventually there's so much there I have to get up to write it down.

Derek Haas: I have a time of day in which I know I'm at my best . . . the morning. Then I turn off the Internet and get to work.

Michael Brandt: I find the right music and turn it up loud. Writing for me comes in bursts, and a great burst of forty-five minutes is usually better than five hours of forced typing.

Jim Kouf: I do a lot of thinking about one hour before I get out of bed or before I go to sleep, but it can happen anywhere. I never leave home without a notepad.

Aline Brosh McKenna: I wish I had rituals like other writers. But I have found over the years that there's no summoning the muse, there's sitting in chairs.

Terry Rossio: The only odd thing I do is take long drives. I'll intentionally schedule a two-, three-, or four-hour drive when I need to make a lot of progress on a project. Sometimes I'll pick up a Stephen King book. For some reason, the rhythm of his writing, the casual ease of it, helps me believe that I can do it, too. Best not to combine these two techniques.

Welcoming the Muse

Aha! Light bulb! Eureka! Out of nowhere, a great idea just struck you while you were pumping gas into your car. Don't let it escape. Do you have anything to record it on?

25. Record Your Ideas as Soon as They Appear

Dig the well before you are thirsty.
—CHINESE PROVERB

Good ideas come and go quickly, so most of our accomplished writers don't let them escape. They record everything—random thoughts, observations, character sketches, overheard bits of conversation. Some use tape recorders, others notebooks or whatever piece of paper is lying around. Others feel self-conscious talking into a tape recorder; they'd rather write ideas directly on paper. Since the advent of cell phones, many find it convenient to call their answering machine, especially when an idea happens to strike while they're driving.

Steven de Souza: I believe in free association. I always carry a bunch of three-by-five cards where I write ideas that come to me—bits of dialogue or odd observations. Eventually, a couple of them will collide to form a whole new idea, or they'll achieve a critical mass, and a light bulb will flash in my head and I'll say, that's a story.

Akiva Goldsman: I don't do anything. I just try to remember it. I believe good ideas stay so if I forget one, it probably wasn't a good idea. The danger is that everything seems good in the moment. The question is, does it last? Does it live with you?

Amy Holden Jones: I have several notebooks all over the place, and a scrapbook in my computer where I jot down ideas as they occur to me when I'm writing. I pop into it periodically and find that I forgot about a particular detail or line of dialogue. If I'm in the car, I try to remember it, but I often forget it. Small and forgettable ideas are meaningless. What matters are the big ideas of theme and plot and characters. If you suddenly get a solution that comes out of the blue, you'll remember it if it's important.

Terry Rossio: I write my ideas down on "stickies" on my MacBook Pro. I like stickies. Something about them fools me into thinking that I'm not really writing, so there's no stress. I often forgo the screenwriting programs and write first drafts on stickies.

Raising the Idea to Maturity

Now you can let your left-brain take over and judge what you've come up with. You also need to put it in some kind of order and know where you want to go before you start.

26. Outline Your Story

> *Know where you're going.*
>
> —BILLY WILDER

Three thousand years ago, Aristotle said in *Poetics*, "As for the story, whether the poet takes it ready-made or constructs it for himself, he should first sketch its general outline, and then fill in the episodes and amplify in detail." Outlining is one of the most universally accepted habits among writers. It is very much like constructing a human skeleton bone by bone before applying flesh, blood, nerves, and skin.

Ron Bass: When I feel I have enough critical mass, I put an outline together. I take out three sheets of paper—Act One, Two, and Three—and I write down every scene, usually from the top down and the bottom up. I usually know what my first scenes are and what my act out [act break] is so I figure out the scenes that lead to that. I don't necessarily know the order of all scenes but I try different ways.

Then I start plugging in the numbers, see if they work, move them around. Eventually, I end up with a first act that has fifteen or sixteen scenes, and I immediately page budget it to see how long these scenes will be. I can figure out which scenes will be two pages and which ones will be longer, so I get an idea how long my act is. If it's sixty-seven pages long, I know I have a problem. If it's fifteen pages, I know I need more scenes.

I do this with the second act and the third, eventually getting an outline in shape. Now I go back and look at all the notes I have and figure out if I want to keep them or get rid of them. If the note stays, I have to put a scene number [on it] because it has to go somewhere. If there's no place for it to go, I get rid of it. Next, I do what I call "blocking," which is putting together everything I might want to have in Scene One. It could be anything—dialogue, setting, tone, or what the character is wearing. Once I'm done blocking and all the scenes are numbered according to my outline, I know when I'll start writing, so I make up my schedule. I have my little chart of all the days. I figure out, for instance, "Okay, today I can write Scene One; tomorrow I can write Two and Three, they're really short; next day, I'll start Four, it's really long, and I'll finish it the day after that and start Five, etc." Then I start writing. Of course, my outline will change. The second it does, I stop writing and reschedule according to my new outline.

Gerald DiPego: First, I keep testing the idea in my head, trying to draw it out into a beginning, middle, and end, thinking about what it really means, what it's about. If it passes the test, I'll flesh it out in broad strokes, hitting the highlights of the story with the elements that have inspired me, that I've had in my head for a while. I'll think it through by running the movie in my head over and over, so that each time I come back to the outline, it fleshes out more and more. By the time I have thought it through, including what my characters are like, I'll have a twelve- to fifteen-page outline. That's when I'm almost ready to write, because by then I've really seen the movie in my head, scene by scene. But before I start to write, I'll do a character check— ask myself whether I really know these people, what they love, what they hate, what they're afraid of, what they want, how do they move through a room, what are their voices. I don't start writing until I feel I have a unique personality, tone of voice, and pattern of speech for each character.

Tony Gilroy: I definitely outline. I spend a lot of time prepping and sketching, where I'm very messy and loose, often ending up with hundreds of different files, which could be scenes, character notes, or dialogue—mostly a lot of dialogue. I tend to plot through dialogue. If I don't hear people talking, I can't move forward. I probably write a couple of hundred messy pages of notes before I start a script. But when I start the script, I get very precise.

Derek Haas: Michael and I get together ahead of time to work out our outlines. We'll end up with a seven- to ten-page treatment that pretty much contains all the beats of the story. And we usually divide it into "emotional plot" and "actual plot." We'll refine that back and forth via e-mail after we've put it down on paper. Then we feel like we're ready.

Michael Brandt: When you're working on an assignment, you have to have an outline, because the studio wants to know what you're going to be writing. It isn't terribly detailed, so you can still have inspiration as you write. But outlining does solve the big issues of the script ahead of time.

Amy Holden Jones: It depends on the project. Sometimes you're given a book to adapt, sometimes it's an assignment and you have to come up with a story, and sometimes you get an idea of your own. For instance, *Mystic Pizza* started with the actual restaurant and I thought it would be a great title for a movie. So a title is a good way to start. I usually start with a theme, then I think about the characters. The reason I start with the theme first is because the nature of the characters will illustrate and reflect on that theme.

A theme is not necessarily complicated. For example, *Indecent Proposal* explored whether money can buy love and what is its corrupting effect on love. I had always wanted to do a movie about a marriage over time and the violation of trust and friendship. After thinking about the characters, I start to think about the ending and I begin to outline in broad strokes with the basic three-act structure. It's the same process I go through to prepare for a pitch, especially for a book adaptation, because novels are not readily adaptable, so you have to find a way to tell the story in a three-act structure. I have to admit, though, that I often depart from it once I start writing.

Nicholas Kazan: Once the story fleshes out, I start developing an outline until I don't know what happens next and I stop. I go back to writing notes for a few more weeks until the story becomes clearer and then write another outline without looking at the first one. I start from scratch. If you've ever had the experience of losing a document after a computer crash and having to rewrite it without looking at the original, what you often find is that you've remembered the best stuff and forgotten what was problematic. That's why I try to do another outline from memory. Eventually, I go back and look at the original just in case I overlooked a minor detail. Once I have an outline that goes all the way through, I'll start getting anxious and ready to start.

Bill Marsilii: I write a very detailed outline, usually between twenty and twenty-five pages. Each scene has a slug line in caps that tells me what it is, followed by a prose paragraph about anything and everything I know about that scene, often transcribed from the index card. But right before it, I'll have a line that says, "Establish:" and the key things that must be established in that scene and the reason that scene must be there.

Ideally, a good scene should accomplish several things at once, so writing the establishing line helps me see where a scene might be weak. For instance, if I only have one line written, like "Establish that my character is funny," I may wonder why I have an entire scene just for that. I could show him being funny in another scene. So this helps to highlight the weak scenes.

Scott Rosenberg: When I feel ready, I sit down with a legal pad, number it one through seventy, and I write a simple sentence for each beat of the story. I end up with an outline where I'll know what my first-act break and my second-act break are. Of course, this outline will constantly change, and I tool with it for about a week.

When I feel it's in good shape, I'll sit down and start to write. The cool thing is that you have this legal pad in front of you, and as you write each scene, you check off these numbers and get this real sense of completion.

Terry Rossio: All writers outline. Some just do it the slow way, writing multiple drafts without outlines to discover their outline. As for paradigms, I believe in beginning, middle, and end, not necessarily in that order. Pretty much every paradigm fits every movie. That stuff is all analysis after the fact. I do believe that a feature film script is composed of between twenty-four and twenty-eight sequences. Because a film is a physical thing, shot on different locations, there commonly turns out to be a location-based aspect to film stories. If the writer takes that into consideration from the start, the work is properly constrained, like a playwright understanding the realities of a story unfolding on the stage.

Ed Solomon: I work in generations. By this I mean, I get the idea and I can easily fit it on a page, often even in a paragraph, then I stop. I start again a few days later and try to expand it to a few pages. Then when I feel I can tell the story, I try to develop a more detailed outline, always making sure I leave enough room to discover things. And then I get to that point of inevitability when I just have to start writing. It's not really a feeling that I want to write it, but more like I have no choice. It just starts itself.

27. Discover a Few Scenes at a Time

> *Discovery consists of looking at the same thing as*
> *everyone else and thinking something different.*
> —ALBERT SZENT-GYORGYI

Just as most screenwriters like to outline and know where they're going in the story, there are some who prefer the more organic and spontaneous process of discovering moments of narrative and character as they write. An analogy would be driving from Los Angeles to New York. You could map out all the details, pit stops, miles driven per day, touristy sights to visit along the way, and exact time of arrival. Or, armed with a compass and only knowing you must head east, you could just let the highways guide you, as you discover the United States. Either way is valid, depending on how much time you have.

Jim Kouf: I usually start jotting things down, bits of dialogue, theme, character, key words, and try to build things until I have a rough outline. But many times, when I'm just writing for myself, I'll just start writing a script, because for me it's the same process of writing an outline, except with an outline you think in broader strokes and in the script you have to think in details. So I figure I might as well write the script. I can always throw it away and start over, but at least I'm thinking through all the details that I'd have had to think through anyway with an outline.

Eric Roth: I'm not a big outliner. I'll outline just two or three scenes ahead, but I'll let the writing kind of take me in different directions sometimes. Let's assume I'm starting. The first scene I'll know backward and forward. You really want to grab the reader and bring them into some world they haven't been in before that's unique, that'll pique their interest and excite them. Then I know what the next three or four scenes are. When I get to the fourth scene, I'll know what the next three or four are. This leaves a little room for discovery. Sometimes characters take me to different places I wasn't aware of before.

CHAPTER 7

CREATING A WRITING ENVIRONMENT

28. Have a Favorite Writing Space

Appealing workplaces are to be avoided. One wants a room with no view, so imagination can meet memory in the dark.
—ANNIE DILLARD

It helps to create a space where you feel comfortable being, creating, and writing for long periods of time, and where you tell your mind, "I'm here to write."

Ron Bass: Whenever I can, I like to write outdoors, whether in my backyard or in parks. But if I'm writing indoors, I like a small space, a cozy kind of feel, like a cocoon. I've actually written scenes sitting in the passenger seat of my car, parked some place, like when I go to the park and it's too cold. Instead of going home, I'd sit in my car and finish the scene. Nobody bothers me, and since it's such a small, confined space, I can't do anything but write.

Gerald DiPego: About three years ago, I realized a dream of having my own writing studio because I had been working in a makeshift office in a bedroom. So I took some backyard space and built a small studio. It's nothing fancy but it's my complete world with all my books, file cabinets, artwork, a nice long table where I write, and only my favorite things that inspire me. I also collect toy soldiers, so I have a cabinet with my collections. It's nice to have things by your side that can take you back to your childhood.

Tony Gilroy: I've never been much of a public writer, though I've had luck breaking a story with pen and paper at bars all over the world. But actual writing, I've always done in private offices. I've done a lot of hotel writing. I've spent a huge amount of my life writing in hotel rooms. I don't like to write in the room I sleep in, so I always try to get a suite, and another peculiarity is that I prefer a banquet chair to a desk chair. I've gotten really good at asking for a banquet chair in many different languages. And I usually rearrange the furniture to my liking. And if I know I'll be writing for a couple of days, I bring an external keyboard I feel comfortable with. And a printer. I print a lot. I'm a paper abuser. I like to see things on paper.

Akiva Goldsman: Right now, I'm writing in my dining room. I always write on a laptop computer. I have an old, clunky one that I really like and a tiny one that I take on planes. Whenever possible I need to have a view and be able to see out. Even when I lived in Brooklyn, I could still look up at the sky over the top of the buildings. So I sit at my dining-room table facing the windows that look out over the city and just tap, tap, tap.

Amy Holden Jones: I think it's pretty unusual: I have a zero gravity chair, so I write completely relaxed in an almost horizontal position. My chair is positioned so that when I look out the window I can see down a canyon to the ocean. I write directly into a laptop computer that sits on a portable desk positioned perfectly over me.

Scott Rosenberg: I can write anywhere but not outdoors. I write directly into a computer. I have this huge bulletin board against the wall that has pictures of everything, from photographs of my family and friends to pictures of Steve McQueen, the southern sheriff from a James Bond movie, Heather Graham, *A Clockwork Orange*, some quotes, basically different sources of inspiration that I can look at anytime.

Eric Roth: I write upstairs in an office in my home. It's fairly dark. I like it dark. I don't want to be distracted.

Michael Schiffer: I'm very fortunate to have a studio apartment that acts as my office on the ninth floor of a building in Venice, overlooking the ocean. I call it my writing module. It's very modest, nothing fancy, lots of natural lighting, a desk with my typewriter and another desk that I handwrite on, with a picture of Henry Miller behind me, and lots of reference books. I like to proofread in public, in a coffee shop with lots of ambient noise. I've generally been working so long at my desk at that point that I need the break. I need to be in some other environment to see what I've written clearly and objectively.

Robin Swicord: [My writing place] opens into a garden so I don't feel like I'm in jail. I have lots of natural lighting, a lamp on my desk, and my books all around me, which makes it easy for me to look up stuff. I know not everyone can have the luxury of having a room of their own to just write but I think it's important not to sleep in the room where you work. One of the hardest things for me when I was living in a one-room apartment in New York was that I could never sleep very well because my work would be right at the foot of my bed waiting for me. It's important to give the mind a rest, be able to turn it off and go to another refuge, especially if you work at night.

29. Be Comfortable with Your Writing Tools

Nothing is more sacred to a craftsman than his equipment,
and no one can tell you which are best for you.
—Kenneth Atchity, *A Writer's Time*

All you need to communicate is something to write with—a pencil, a pen, a paintbrush, a computer, and something to write on—paper, a canvas, or a printer. No one tool means success. As you'll see, writers have their own preferences. The important thing is that they're comfortable with them because comfort means relaxation, and relaxation means higher creativity. It doesn't matter what tools you use, as long as they help you write. You can even delude yourself into thinking you must have the latest screenwriting software in order to start your script.

Ron Bass: I write with pencil on three-hole punched paper, which goes in a loose-leaf notebook. In the notebook with my current script, there are two pencil cases clipped inside—one contains newly sharpened pencils, the other receives the pencils that become dull from writing. I never write on a legal pad because I like to be able to move pages around where they belong in the outline.

Ed Solomon: I like big white boards on the wall where I can write with different colored markers. I used to write on notepads and transcribe into the computer, but now I find I can think more with my fingers on the keyboard, though I find it just as easy to procrastinate on the keyboard as I do on the notepad.

Robin Swicord: I love my computer. I write directly into it but I also have a notepad on my desk because often, when I want to write dialogue and I don't want to think about margins and the cursor flashing, I'll jot down what these voices are saying. Sometimes, there's a conversation going on and I just want my pen to fly on the page. Then I'll go back to my computer screen and craft the scene with what I just jotted down.

30. Have a Favorite Time to Write

Now this is very important and can hardly be emphasized too
strongly: You have decided to write at four o'clock,
and at four o'clock write you must!
                                              —DOROTHEA BRANDE

One could also say "regular" or "productive" time to write because the periods of time in which our screenwriters usually write may not necessarily be their "favorite." But it certainly is when their creative output is of the highest quality. The times differ widely among writers, although most prefer writing in the morning, starting the day with a fresh mind after a good night's sleep and unencumbered by life's daily demands. But the writing time you establish should suit your individual creative style.

Leslie Dixon: I'm always better in the afternoon and best still in the evening, but I probably wouldn't be married if I wrote at night. Once in a blue moon when my husband is working at night, I'll rush to the computer and write. I'd go to bed at three in the morning and sleep until ten if the world would let me. I become progressively more alert and clever with every hour after noon that passes. The minute the sun goes down, I'm fully alive. That's why I generally do all the mundane things after I get up in the morning, like read scripts or get my e-mail correspondence out of the way.

Tony Gilroy: If I'm on a roll, early morning is usually good because it's quiet. And when I have to, I can write around the clock. But my absolute sweet spot is always late afternoon, early evening. The bulk of my career has been built between three o'clock and seven-thirty P.M.

Amy Holden Jones: I usually write in the afternoon and evening. In the morning, I exercise and gradually work into the writing by doing other things like reading the newspaper and playing on the computer with e-mail and the Internet.

Bill Marsilii: I do most of my productive writing after midnight. This is actually a habit from my early days when I was working a day job, sometimes two jobs, day and night. The only time I had to write was between two and six A.M., and I started getting used to that. I often got most of my writing done on Thursday nights because I knew I could caffeinate my way through Friday and then crash over the weekend. Even today, when I start a new project, I tend to stay up very late.

Scott Rosenberg: My best hours are between eleven A.M. and four P.M., unless the writing is going really well or I'm in production or I have a deadline, then I write all the time, whenever I can.

Terry Rossio: I write at night, from around ten P.M. to three A.M.

Eric Roth: I like to work in the middle of the night a lot when I'm sort of half asleep. I like to go with the imagery that may come out of dreams. If it's interesting and applies to what I'm writing, I'll find ways to use it. But I usually write at the same time every day. I start at eight or nine in the morning and I find I can be creative for about four hours. In the afternoon, I like to hang out with my kids or go to the races, and then I'll start again at around nine in evening and go until I'm tired or bored. Then I'll wake up in the middle of the night if it's going well. I'll write for about an hour and then take a little nap before waking up for the next day.

Michael Schiffer: I drive into my office and I'm at work between eight and eight-thirty. It's the first focused thing I do each day. I like getting the night's subconscious work or thoughts onto the page. When I sit down at the typewriter and begin, I have all the night's dream work still inside me. I find that if I do things all day long, I don't bring my insides to the table. If I can't work in the morning to start, the day is blown for original writing. The best I can do is edit what's already on the page.

Tom Schulman: I'm always writing by nine in the morning and try to quit at four-thirty. I write from nine until noon, watch CNN for half an hour as I eat my lunch, and then go back to writing from twelve-thirty to four-thirty.

• • •

As you can see, even a well-developed, outlined story doesn't magically turn itself into 110-page screenplay. It still takes hard work. Successful screenwriters are highly disciplined and, like any worker, they keep regular hours. Sure, you may think, "That's easy for them, they've been doing it for years. How can I get some of that discipline to rub off on me?" Let's find out.

PART 3

DISCIPLINE

Applying the Seat of Your Pants to the Seat of the Chair

It is not the same to talk of bulls as to be in the bullring.
—SPANISH PROVERB

CHAPTER 8

THE WRITING HABIT

31. Write Regularly

*I write only when I'm inspired. Fortunately
I'm inspired at nine o'clock every morning.*
—WILLIAM FAULKNER

The difference between successful screenwriters and dreamers is that at the end of the day, successful screenwriters have more pages written than they did the day before. This requires daily writing. Even if you hate to write, even if it takes you a whole day to warm up only to write one page, it's better than no writing at all because if you do it every day, it'll become a habit.

As author Tom Robbins once answered a student's question about inspiration: "I'm always at my desk by ten o'clock, so the muse knows where to find me. Sometimes she comes and sometimes she doesn't, but if she does, I want to be there." So think of writing as something you're required to do every day, like eating, sleeping, and brushing your teeth. You don't have to be inspired to do those things, you just accept them as part of your day. Feel the same about your writing.

Ron Bass: The process of writing is so joyful, so satisfying, so *necessary* for me that I'd do it even if no one else in the world but me was ever going to read it, let alone pay me a dime to do it. Aside from the pleasure I get from interacting with the people I love and care about, writing is the most intense pleasure I could ever have alone.

Leslie Dixon: The physical act of writing is sometimes a pleasure for me, "satisfying" would be a better word. It tends to flow in pockets and usually doesn't last more than a couple of hours at a time. I fall in the crowd who hates to write but loves to have written, like Dorothy Parker.

Akiva Goldsman: Writing is both a pleasure and a struggle. There are times when it's really aversive and unpleasant, and there are times when it's wonderful and fun and magical, but that's not the point. Writing is my job. I'm not a believer of waiting for the muse. You don't put yourself in a mood to go to your nine-to-five job, you just go.

I start in the morning and write all day. Successful writers don't wait for the muse to fill themselves unless they're geniuses. I'm not a genius. I'm smart, I have some talent, and I have a lot of stubbornness. I persevere. I was by no means the best writer in my class in college. I'm just the one who is still writing.

Nicholas Kazan: I write every day, but not on weekends, now that I have children. However, if it's a first draft and I need the continuity, it's much easier to write every day, even if I work only a couple of hours and don't get a lot done. It's a way of visiting the world of this screenplay, so when I come back to it on Monday morning, there's no adjustment to make. If I start writing after two days away without contact, it's more difficult to re-enter the script.

Scott Rosenberg: It's just automatic pilot, a habit. You just wake up, get your coffee, glance at the paper, sit down, and just go. Sure, you have bad days. I've had days where I sat there for an hour and a half and nothing came. Then, I just say, "I know better than to force it. Tomorrow's another day."

32. Face the Blank Page

A professional is someone who can do great work when he doesn't feel like it.

—ALISTAIR COOKE

Often, facing the blank page, staring at the blinking cursor until words pop into your mind, is the hardest part of writing. As Gene Fowler once said, "Writing is easy. You just sit staring at the blank sheet of paper until drops of blood form on your forehead."

Because writing is so agonizing, most writers are always on the lookout for tricks to help them deal with this crucial step of the writing process. Some like to read their favorite writer's work to get inspired, others like to listen to energetic music to get their blood pumping. Many like to exercise or take long walks, while some work to never have to face a blank page. They simply go over the previous pages, rewriting and polishing, so that by the time they get to end, they just keep going where they left off the previous day.

Ron Bass: I'm a great believer in preparation. I work fourteen hours a day, spending six hours writing the script I'm working on, then I return phone calls and take meetings for two or three hours, whatever I have to do, and I spend four hours a day developing my next script, from the initial idea to all the other stages of it. So by the time I write "Fade out" on the current script, I set the current notebook aside—everything is in a separate notebook because I don't own a computer, I move over to the next notebook and I take out every page of notes. The first scene of that next script is already completely outlined and page-budgeted, with blocking and notes for every scene. This way you never start with a blank page. Preparation is the key, because most people are eager to write that first scene; they can't wait, but they don't know what the rest of the script is about. You can't write that first scene without knowing the last scene, and the scenes in the middle, because it isn't just about what you think of that scene; it's where that scene has to take you, what that scene means to everything that follows.

Gerald DiPego: I hear writers complain about the blank page all the time. I consider myself lucky because I actually enjoy it. When there's a story going inside me and I'm writing a screenplay or a novel, it's so alive in me that it feels good to get it out on paper.

Tony Gilroy: Except for the first day's work on a script, I never really have to look at a blank page. I like to edit the final printout of a day's writing right before going to sleep, so in the morning, I have something to work on, which builds up steam for that day's writing.

Derek Haas: I re-read whatever pages came right before the scene I'm about to work on, then I push forward from there.

Amy Holden Jones: Exercising before writing helps because it makes your blood flow and you feel more energetic to face the task at hand. But it's usually a struggle because I don't do enough pre-planning. I usually work really hard on my first draft, which is like an outline, and when I know what I want to do, I'll start over again.

Nicholas Kazan: I love the blank page. It's a world of possibilities. I have no problems in the morning because I prepared the night before. I learned this trick from Hemingway, who used to stop writing in the middle of a sentence because he knew his mind would work on what came afterward and finish the sentence the next day.

Similarly, I try not to write to the point of exhaustion, where I've written everything I could possibly write that day. If I've written ten pages and I'm satisfied with them, and it's one o'clock and I still have energy to work a couple of hours, I'll play around with the scenes I'll be writing the next day. I'll rough them out, jot down images and bits of dialogue in a really primitive way. Sometimes I'll look at it the next day and it's no good, but more often, it's really good because there's no pressure on me. So there's no re-entry problem because I'm sort of rewriting and polishing what I did the day before.

Andrew W. Marlowe: When you're an aspiring writer, summoning the muse is a luxury. For professional writers, it's a necessity. For me, the hardest thing is to sit down on the chair and start to commit. When you're thinking about it in your head, there's not a sense of committing. It's like dating a whole bunch of people, but when you're writing it on the page, it's like getting married. Yes, you can always change things on the page, but everybody finds their own way to feel comfortable sitting on the chair and pressing the keys on the keyboard. For me, it's having my coffee, walking around, and finally landing on an idea, a notion, an angle of attack, something compelling that makes me want to shape it on paper.

Bill Marsilii: To get in the mood, I have a wide variety of environmental CDs. The ones I end up playing most are thunderstorms and rain showers. Part of that comes from my days in New York where I lived in a noisy area and I had to put on headphones to drown out the distractions. But music would distract me too much, so these ambient sounds help me get into a flow state. Whenever it actually rains here, I'm in heaven.

Aline Brosh McKenna: I wish there was something that made the cursor go by itself but ultimately it's all about sitting in the chair. You just have to do it. You just have to keep doing it, and you just have to print it and read it and keep doing it. There are so many things that are more enticing than sitting in the chair, but at the end of the day, that's what you need to do. It's the essence of the job.

Terry Rossio: When the deadline is really upon me, and I must sit and write for many hours straight, I'll play a single song, set to repeat. One song, over and over. This creates, over time, an odd, hypnotic atmosphere, as if time is not moving at all.

Eric Roth: Mostly, I have something I've been wanting to write down, something I wrote in the middle of the night, a note or a sketched-out scene, and I just sit down and read the thing. All of a sudden, I'm immersed in it. Reading over your previous day's work gives you momentum.

Michael Schiffer: What puts me in the mood to write are desperation and fear. I had it when I had no money and no credits, and now I've got a family to support. I like writing first thing in the morning, starting with that first "Okay, I'm alive and awake and now I'm going to work."

Tom Schulman: I don't really think about it because it's become a habit. At nine o'clock, the computer is on, I'm ready, I say to myself, "I really don't want to do this today," and I just start. A teacher once said to me, "You have to go to work just like a grocer. You unlock the doors at whatever hour, turn the sign over, walk in and start working."

Ed Solomon: I love the blank page. It's like arriving at Community Chest in Monopoly. You don't know what's going to be there when you turn it over. I don't know why writers complain about it. I find it harder to stare at a page that has words on it. The blank page is a big open invitation. The other great thing is not having a rigid schedule to write during the day so that I can just write at a more organic pace, and slow it down or speed it up as I need to.

Robin Swicord: I'm writing all the time. I have to put myself in the mood to do other things. My mind turns to what I'm working on the way it turns to my children or my husband when I see them again after a day apart. It's a reunion when I sit back down to the page.

33. Write to Music

Music has the capacity to touch the innermost reaches of the soul, and music gives flight to the imagination.

—PLATO

Many writers use music to put or keep themselves in the mood to write. Music undoubtedly has an effect on the brain. Studies have shown that it can help relieve stress and aid in relaxation. Fast-paced music with a heavy beat can have stimulating effects, increasing heartbeat and blood flow, while some studies have suggested that listening to classical music helps increase cognitive functioning.

Ron Bass: I usually write in parks, but when I have to write indoors, I play jazz in the background. How loud or how soft depends on how I feel at that moment. I like to play the same CDs over and over because I like the music to disappear. When I introduce a new CD into the mix, it can take my attention for a while, so I like to hear something that's so familiar I don't even know I'm hearing it. It becomes part of the atmosphere, creating a kind of warm, cozy, homelike feeling of relaxation.

Steven de Souza: I play music all the time, usually soundtracks from movies similar to the genre I'm writing.

Derek Haas: I always have music on when I'm writing. It lets my wife know not to bother me. I like to put on albums I've heard a thousand times, so I don't have to concentrate on the music; it just bleeds into whatever I'm working on at the time. Things with driving beats certainly get me going: Rush, Rage Against the Machine, Pearl Jam.

Nicholas Kazan: The last couple of years, I've started writing to music, mostly classical music or Gregorian chants. I don't like soundtracks because they're usually hyped up. I need something more constant and neutral. I find it's a wonderful aid that sort of massages the right hemisphere of my brain.

34. Write in Silence

There are times when silence has the loudest voice.
—LEROY BROWNLOW

There are just as many writers who like to write in complete silence because music distracts them. Silence allows them to quiet their mind and focus completely on the scene at hand.

Leslie Dixon: I can't write with music on because I'm musical. I'd start thinking how interesting the bass line is, or how awful is that disco chord. I don't even have music in the car anymore because it's so distracting.

Amy Holden Jones: I write in complete silence, although I often leave CNN on in the background so that if I get stuck, I can look up at it.

Eric Roth: I don't listen to music while I write, but I'll listen to different kinds of music on an iPod while I walk every morning. Sometimes, a songwriter will articulate some idea or feeling that may apply to what I'm writing.

Robin Swicord: I don't write to music because I'm easily swayed by it. Sometimes, I'll put music on when I'm sitting down, reading yesterday's pages and thinking about what I want to do today, especially if it's a piece of music I associate with the emotion of what I'm working on. It tends to unlock the door a little bit and helps you focus on the business at hand.

35. Exercise

If you are seeking creative ideas, go out walking.
Angels whisper to a man when he goes for a walk.
—RAYMOND INMON

Exercise is a great way to get the blood flowing. We all know that aerobic exercise helps enhance creativity and sharper thinking. After all, your brain depends on efficient blood flow. Some writers exercise before writing, aware of its effect on their writing during the day, while others do it after writing, or else they'd be too tired to write. Still, since the effect of exercising lasts well into the next day, one could argue that they actually exercise the day before writing.

Walking seems to be a screenwriter's favorite form of exercise. Evidence shows that when walking, blood circulation increases, but the leg muscles don't need the extra oxygen that more strenuous exercises require. This means that walking oxygenates the brain more effectively than other forms of exercise.

Ron Bass: I try to exercise every day. I ride thirty minutes on a stationary bike as soon as I wake up, and I lift weights every other day. I also take long walks with my wife on the weekends.

Steven de Souza: I try to exercise three times a week after I'm done writing, around midday. When I was doing television and I'd hit a rough spot where my brain wasn't as sharp, I'd ride a bicycle around the lot until my blood started flowing again. I still do that if I feel sluggish.

Gerald DiPego: It's important to clear your head and restore yourself, so a long walk is helpful for regenerating ideas.

Leslie Dixon: I exercise after my kid goes to bed because the house is really quiet and nobody's bugging me. I also take baths almost every night before I go to bed, which is sort of meditative, although I take them not to be relaxed enough to attract thoughts, but to make them go away.

Tony Gilroy: I like to exercise in the morning. I'm a gym rat, but for me it's contemplative. I constantly strategize about all my calls and the people I have to talk to that day, or I'll be thinking about the story I'm developing or the scenes I'll be writing later that day. So my shower at eleven A.M. really feels like the culmination of my day, where I'll know exactly what I'll be doing later.

Amy Holden Jones: I exercise in the morning. I walk, I golf, I do Pilates and yoga.

Nicholas Kazan: I exercise at the end of the day. I run, swim, and bike.

Scott Rosenberg: I exercise after I write. I go to the gym and do yoga, weights, and run on the treadmill.

Tom Schulman: Walking is best. Any physical activity helps. For instance, I'm often full of ideas the day after my wife and I go dancing.

Robin Swicord: I usually take a forty-minute walk in the morning before I write. The process of getting ready to go to my desk begins when I walk. If I do something more vigorous, like swimming or an aerobic class, I'll do it after I write.

36. Take Naps and Relax

I shut my eyes in order to see.

—PAUL GAUGUIN

Taking a break once in a while allows you to park your mind in neutral and be in touch with your inner thoughts. Writers often feel blocked because of stress. Muscles are tight, energy doesn't flow smoothly. It's through rest and relaxation, meditation, or other distractions that they're able to recharge, focus on their thoughts, and often put their inner critic and racing conscious thoughts to sleep, thus freeing their mind to wander without pressures.

Steven de Souza: I take naps, but not on a regular basis. Sometimes, I'll wake up at four in the morning for a call of nature and I'll have a flash of an idea, and I'm so excited that I don't want to wait three more hours until my official start time. So I'll start writing, but by nine o'clock I'll be fried. That's when short naps really help to get you through the day. I'm fortunate in that I'm one of those people who can fall asleep at any moment, like a light switch.

Nicholas Kazan: I do take naps about three times a week. Writing is so debilitating that I find it very productive to take a fifteen- to twenty-minute nap in the afternoon.

Tom Schulman: I'm a big believer in naps. Midafternoon, I usually lie down on the floor for about twelve to twenty minutes.

37. Be Nutritionally Aware

> *Food is an important part of a balanced diet.*
> —Fran Lebowitz

If you know how different kinds of food and beverage affect your thinking, you can get into the habit of eating and drinking the right things for your brain—and your creative process. Our mentors are aware of the effects of food, drink, and drugs on their creative thinking. It doesn't mean their nutritional habits are the healthiest, just that they're aware of the effects, and they adopt whatever works for them. Proceed at your own risk.

Steven de Souza: I'm not a junk-food eater and I've never had much of a sweet tooth. But there is something that works like cocaine for me called Poppycock—sort of designer Cracker Jack. Interestingly, they originally sold it in film cans. I'm also a coffee drinker, so between the two, I could go all night if I had to.

Amy Holden Jones: I don't drink coffee or tea, but chocolate around three P.M. usually helps.

Nicholas Kazan: I drink a lot of tea during the day. Coffee is too much for me.

Scott Rosenberg: I have one cup of coffee in the morning to get started. I drink water all the time and try to have some carrot juice once in a while, but I don't snack or have any sugary things while I'm doing it.

Tom Schulman: All I have in the morning right when I start is one cup of decaffeinated coffee with hot chocolate in it, and I drink a lot of water throughout the day. I have a very light breakfast, usually a bowl of cereal with some fruit on top, and a light lunch, maybe a small sandwich and an apple. I find that if I eat heavy, I get tired in the afternoon.

38. Write Through Your Fears

> *Courage is not the absence of fear, but rather the judgment*
> *that something else is more important than fear.*
> —AMBROSE REDMOON

This whole industry runs on fear. Fear of saying yes to a potential box-office flop, fear of missing out on a hot script, fear of being found out and never working again.

As writers, we all have to face our fears—"What if I write something awful? What if I'm criticized? What if I don't have enough talent?"—and write anyway. Delaying writing because you think you're just not good enough won't get you closer to a finished draft. What helps is not worrying about making your first draft a masterpiece. Just think of it as a draft that no one will see until you want them to. You can make it perfect later. Put it on the page. As Sol Saks once said, "The worst thing you write is better than the best thing you didn't write."

Ron Bass: Even today when I have a meeting at a studio and somebody says, "Ron, we don't think the quality of this piece is up to your standard, it's just not what we expected," it still devastates me. I just go home and feel really, really bad. Even when my team says, "Oh, you're a great writer, you're brilliant, etcetera," you still question your talent. Dustin Hoffman once said to me, "Every role is going to be my last; this is the one when they'll realize I can't act, I never could act; I will be found out, and this time I will fall off the tightrope, and they'll tear me to pieces and I'll never be allowed to act again."

You always have these fears because there's no objective standard. Even when your movie comes out, you realize it wasn't all you, it was Julia Roberts or a hundred other factors. Or your movie doesn't get made and the next one is a failure. It's hard to be in an industry where people alternately tell you you're brilliant and they didn't like something. Who's right and who's wrong? But you don't really want to give up your insecurity, because it's tied to the requisite humility. If you're not humble about the quality of your work and embrace the fear that it's not good enough, that everything that comes out of your mouth isn't just golden because you said it and you're famous, then you're dead.

Jim Kouf: My only writing fear is trying not to repeat what I've already done. I'm always thinking, "How can I do this better?" The toughest thing is to keep coming up with original ideas. You have to go through a hundred ideas to find the one that's right. That takes a lot of thought and a lot of trying. You just keep writing. The other fear is, "When will they stop paying me?"

Bill Marsilii: I've been comforted somewhat by seeing how many writers I admire use the phrase, "working up the courage to write." I've come to accept that part of my process is to face these first weeks of dread where I'm staying up all night getting virtually nothing done and fearing that this will be the project where I never get past this point, that this will be the one where the muse never comes, even though I know in my rational brain that I always get past it. It's part of the process. You have to keep showing up at the keyboard.

Tom Schulman: I wish I could find a way to enjoy the process more, because the fears are part of what makes it so excruciating. The only way you overcome them is by just writing and trying to make it better every day. I may not be able to make it great on a given day, but I can make it a little better every day.

Robin Swicord: My only big fear about writing is that I'm so odd that what fascinates me, the things I'm giving myself to completely, will turn out to be of no interest to anyone else. It will be so personal and idiosyncratic that no one will think it's funny and no one will feel sad when they get to that part and I'll be the only one to care. But then I say, "What the heck, I'll just amuse myself."

39. Silence Your Inner Critic

If you hear a voice within you saying,
"You are not a painter," then by all means paint,
and that voice will be silenced.
—Vincent van Gogh

The inner critic is that voice inside of you that constantly judges your work, criticizing your choice of words, ridiculing your characters, and laughing at your scenes. This inhibits your creative flow and makes you feel inferior as a writer, which is often the main cause of procrastination and writer's block.

To write regularly, you must be able to silence your inner critic, though not forever. You want it in the rewriting phases, just not in the important first draft. So make a deal with it: "I promise to let you be in charge when I'm done with my first draft, but only if you take a break long enough to let me finish my first draft."

Tony Gilroy: I can't silence him. Though I'm not sure I'd want to these days, because that's what challenges me to do good work. He's part of my quality control, my perfectionism.

Derek Haas: Most of the time, I'm just writing to impress Michael. If I impress him, then I know the studio or producers are going to like it too . . . at least, most of the time.

Michael Brandt: My inner critic is Derek. That sounds weird.

Laeta Kalogridis: My husband is my editor, and my biggest critic; my inner one doesn't hold a candle. I just listen to him. When he says it sucks, it probably does, and when he says it's great, I breathe a huge sigh of relief. A good editor is the most important thing you can have, to keep yourself from wandering off into your own head and never coming out.

Andrew W. Marlowe: I've not silenced my inner critic; I have become a partner with it by telling it that it has value, but just at a time and place of my choosing. I tell it, "Look, this is not going out the door without your giving it a thorough scrub. But right now, you're not useful to me. You know stuff is not going to be good right away. It's part of the process. So leave me alone. When I'm ready, you can come back and tell me it's not good enough."

Aline Brosh McKenna: I look at it differently. It's about being in touch with your inner audience member. It's about turning on the part of your brain that responds to things emotionally. Too many writers make decisions from the outside in, based on what you think should happen or what you saw in other movies. I try to disable this left-brain part so that I can experience things emotionally, so that I can react to things in the story as an audience might.

Scott Rosenberg: I used to have this inner critic, but I got rid of him long ago. A professor once said to me, "Remember, no one will ever see what you're writing until you want them to see it." This really freed me up to just write. It's like playing jazz guitar and you're just riffing, and the stuff that sounds really good is the stuff you record. The rest of it just floated away up into the cosmos. You'll just be paralyzed if you labor over every sentence because it has to be perfect. That's a dangerous habit. It should be vomited out as fast as you can get it out. Nobody ever has to see it. Then finesse it, massage it, sweeten it, and do everything you can to make it better.

Terry Rossio: I love my inner critic! I'm not a writer so much as a rewriter. My inner critic is the only way I can elevate my writing beyond my own meager talent.

Eric Roth: I only know what is bogus and what is real, but my inner critic doesn't paralyze me. If something doesn't work, I just try something else. That's one of the main advantages of working with a computer, because I can switch things so easily.

Robin Swicord: I don't let the critic write while I'm writing, but I move between the two boats pretty fluidly. When I go over my material, I'm reading critically. When I sit down to write after I've given myself notes, I send the critic out of the room and I do my writing without anyone looking over my shoulder.

40. Focus Completely on the Task at Hand

The problem with creative writing is essentially one of concentration.
—STEPHEN SPENDER

Successful writers are able to focus their energy on the task at hand. They know their goal and can concentrate on it, experiencing what many call "flow," where they're in that world they've created. Time disappears; they lose all sense of themselves and their environment. While our screenwriters have talked about the importance of chair time, it's also important to cultivate the habit of focusing on your project while you're in your chair.

Michael Brandt: I was always hugely "anti-PDW"—public displays of writing. I always thought anyone in Los Angeles who writes in public is only doing so for the attention. But I've recently spent some time at a local coffee shop, and the din of the place kind of focuses me. Plus I get to show everyone that I'm a writer!

Steven de Souza: I can concentrate to an almost scary degree. I've been lost writing a scene, and then I'll see a hand waving out of the corner of my eye and realize someone has been literally shouting at me to get my attention.

Nicholas Kazan: I read somewhere that the two brain hemispheres switch off their dominance every ninety minutes, and I believe that bursts of automatic writing are triggered when the left hemisphere sets up the writing problem and then, just at the point it's set up, the right hemisphere takes over. This may explain my experiences where I can write for an hour and a half, and after I get up, I literally don't know what I've written.

Aline Brosh McKenna: You just have to do it. I always say it's like having homework, like having had a term paper due for the past twenty years. How do you focus on your term paper when it's due? At some point you just have to do it. But the longer you do it, the easier it gets, though sometimes you have great days where you write eight amazing pages and other days, you have to cut seven of those pages. Which is why this intimidates some people and makes it somewhat of a mysterious process. You don't really know what it's going to take to get there. The only thing I have found that works is to show up with my hammer and nails and just hammer nails all day.

Robin Swicord: I'm not easily distracted unless I want to be. If the writing is not going well that day, I'm not the sort of person that quits and goes shopping. I'm such a Puritan—I'll sit there until four in the afternoon. I never take the easy way out.

41. Work on Several Projects at a Time

> *When I feel difficulty coming on, I switch to another book*
> *I'm writing. When I get back to the problem,*
> *my unconscious has solved it.*
>
> —Isaac Asimov

Having a number of projects going at once, though not necessarily being written at the same time, helps writers handle different problems, like dealing with rejection. Then, getting a project rejected isn't as depressing because you're busy on others. Having several projects also helps keep the creative well fresh. When you run dry of ideas on one, simply switch to another. The most common habit among working screenwriters is to write one screenplay while developing and outlining a few others.

Ron Bass: So many careers flounder because writers go through many drafts of the same script, trying to make it as perfect as they can, and it's still not great, and it doesn't sell, and they feel like failures, and they quit. Far better than rewriting your first script is writing your second script, and your third and fourth, and just keep writing. Make them as different as you can. I rewrite every script as I write it, of course—you go back and forth—but when you're done with the whole script, and you feel it's the best it can be, put it down, forget about it for a while, and begin your second script. It's probably the most important piece of advice I give to writers: Always be planning your next project while you're writing your present one.

Gerald DiPego: It's important to have more than one project, because once you get a script out there, and it's in front of several decision-makers, if you find yourself waiting, it can be very draining. If someone says they'll get back to you in a week, you can figure it will be more like two or three weeks. You can't count on anything when they're so busy. It's always best to put your heart into your next project.

Amy Holden Jones: When I have to, I'll work on one [project] in the morning and one in the afternoon, or I'll work on each on alternate days or weeks. It can be good because you get to move away from stuff and come back to it a little bit fresh.

Nicholas Kazan: When you're stuck on one project, it's okay to concentrate on something else. Many great writers are known to have written their best stuff when they were stuck on something else. So always pay attention when you're going someplace else. Follow it. Play hooky. It doesn't mean that if your brain wants to go to the beach, you go to the beach. If you spend your time at the beach, then you're not a writer. You're a beach bum. But if your mind goes to a different story, write some notes on that story. You may end up writing a great screenplay trying to escape from the original one.

Aline Brosh McKenna: Being a writer is not writing just one script. It's consistently writing good material. One mistake beginners make is writing just one script and five years later, you run into them and they're still dragging around that one script. In those five years, you should have written a bunch more.

42. Avoid Distractions

*Close the door. Unplug the phone. Cheat, lie, disappoint your
pals, if necessary. But get your work done.*
—GARRISON KEILLOR

Because the creative muse is so fickle, it's important to keep interruptions, like the phone, the newspaper, television, the Internet, research, or friends and family, to a minimum.

How do successful screenwriters accomplish this? By limiting any distractions that get in the way, especially in this Internet age, where it gets more and more difficult to focus on any computer task without having the urge to check Facebook and Twitter, read blogs, watch YouTube videos, or play video games.

E-mail notifications are the worst. That constant "ding" every time you receive an e-mail makes it too tempting not to check it. By turning it off and manually checking your e-mail only twice a day, you'll be less distracted. Even better, turn off your Internet connection. You can turn it on again as a reward for having written pages.

Tony Gilroy: When I built my new office last year, I didn't put any Internet in there, though I still had my Blackberry for e-mail. This has made a huge difference in my discipline. I also didn't feel as mentally burnt out at the end of the day as I used to be when I'd constantly get online for everything. I also turn the phone off.

Derek Haas: It's hard. I throw music on and slip into the rhythm. Every now and then, I'll head up to a coffee shop with a pad and pen and no iPad so I won't be distracted.

Laeta Kalogridis: Get some exercise and drink a lot of tea. Turn on the music really loud and close the door. *And turn off the Internet connection!*

Nicholas Kazan: I try not to answer the phone when I work, so I'll return phone calls when I get back home.

Jim Kouf: I'm surrounded by books—medical books, a lot of history, encyclopedias, dictionaries, etcetera. So I don't have to interrupt the creative process for too long [to do the needed research].

Andrew W. Marlowe: When I started out, I used to lock myself in my room and force myself to focus. It's tougher now that I have a family and work at home, but I picked up an idea from my father, who used to have a darkroom. He had a red light outside the room that he switched on whenever he was developing his photos. So I do the same in my office; whenever I need to focus and can't afford to be distracted by my family, I switch on my red light.

Bill Marsilii: I have a little piece of software that basically blanks out the rest of my screen except for whatever program I'm using, so I don't have to see the rest of my files and folders in the background. When I have Final Draft open, it's all I see. Another thing that helps me focus is to change my default desktop wallpaper to a piece of artwork that reminds me of the project I'm currently writing.

For instance, with *Lightspeed* we commissioned artwork from a visual effects artist that we used in our pitch, and I'm using my favorite of those concept paintings as my background. Writing in the wee hours also helps. There's nothing on TV, nobody I know is awake, there's nothing to do, no one I could call, and nowhere to go. All I can do is write.

Aline Brosh McKenna: I try to allow myself a whole day to work with. I do my best work when I'm uninterrupted. So I try not to do any lunches when I'm writing, especially when I'm doing a first draft. If I want to do something social, I'll do breakfast or dinner so I can have most of the day uninterrupted. When you get rolling, you don't want to get up and leave.

Terry Rossio: My only technique is to work late at night, when there's no one around and the phone isn't ringing. But I don't believe in avoiding distractions. I try to be open to life when writing. You don't know what might come along that might trigger an inspiration or a solution. Who's to say that the very thing that is distracting you might not also be the answer screaming at you, the universe trying to help you out?

Robin Swicord: I schedule all my meetings on the same day. I have one special day, usually once a month, where I drive around to all my meetings. All my other days are sacred and devoted to writing.

CHAPTER 9

TIME MANAGEMENT

43. Make the Time to Write

If you have time to whine and complain about something,
you have time to do something about it.
—ANONYMOUS

It's ironic how many aspiring writers say they'd love to write but when they sit down at the computer, they'd rather do anything else—go out with friends, watch TV, play video games. Look at it this way: If the desire to write is not followed by actual writing, then the desire is not to write. Professional screenwriters make writing an excuse not to do other things. They have an all-consuming sense of purpose, and when they're passionate about something, they're dying to do it as often as they can. In short, they make the time, even when they have day jobs, most of them getting up earlier and writing before going to work, or writing at night after working all day.

Laeta Kalogridis: When I had a day job, I wrote late at night and didn't go out much.

Bill Marsilii: Having two jobs, the only time I had was writing after midnight. I was also able to think about my script during my commute, which was close to three hours alone in the car daily, where I was working on my dialogue out loud. When I talk to aspiring writers, I often use the analogy of being in love. If you first meet that special person, where you're thrilled and excited and your IQ jumps twenty points whenever you're around them, you're not going to say, "How can I find the time to date? I work forty hours a week! I'm going to come home, take a shower, and go back out again?! I'm tired! And *Battlestar Galactica* is on!"

No, when you're in love, you'll be writing little love notes at work and wanting to spend all your free time with that person. You'll call her late at night just to say goodnight and hear her voice. Feel that way about your screenplay. Hold out for a soulmate of an idea. When you're in love with what you're writing, you'll find the time to write.

Scott Rosenberg: I always had a day job, so I always wrote nights and weekends. The pact I made with myself was that the minute I made dollar one, I would never again write nights and weekends. Writing would be my job. And it's pretty much what I do now. I wake up and I write between certain hours Monday through Friday. I try to keep in step with the rest of society because most of my friends have day jobs. It's only when I'm particularly excited and it's going well or I have a deadline that I'll write nights and weekends.

Eric Roth: When I had a day job, I found the time to write. I always say to people that if you write two pages a day, five days a week, you'll have a hundred pages in ten weeks. Anyone can find one hour to do two pages, even if you have to do them on a cocktail napkin.

Robin Swicord: There's a wonderful cartoon on our refrigerator of two people at a party. One is a kind of dapper-looking gentleman with an unlined face and a nice big smile, and he's talking to a schlubby, smaller man with big bags under his eyes. And the dapper-looking man is saying, "A writer? I've always wanted to write, but I've never had the time." Everyone has the time to write. The question is, are you willing to turn yourself into the guy with the bags under his eyes in order to make that dream come true? Sure, it's very tiring to have two jobs, but it's a necessary sacrifice if you're a writer. There's no way around that. No one will pay you to write unless you have written something.

44. Have a Schedule

The art of writing is the art of applying the seat of the pants to the seat of the chair.

—MARY HEATON VORSE

We all have dreams, but when you write them down, they become goals. And when you schedule the actions necessary to accomplish your goals, you get things done. Think about how disciplined you become when you have to make a doctor's appointment or an important lunch with a friend. So set an appointment with yourself. Commit to write. Yes, write it down in your calendar and keep that appointment. Not only will you avoid procrastination, but you'll also write regularly, and your brain will eventually rise to the occasion by getting trained to perform at that time.

Ron Bass: I have a writing schedule, but I don't write to a schedule, like nine to twelve every day. Anytime you set up expectations for yourself about anything, you run the risk of feeling like a failure when you don't meet the expectations. What I do is draw a little handwritten chart of all the weeks spanning several months and enter what scene I think I'll write that day, all the way through to the end of the script. The important thing, though, is the second I don't meet that schedule, I change it. I don't like feeling like a failure because I'm four days behind. So I erase it and write a new schedule. If I get ahead of schedule, I don't like to feel too comfortable, so I also change it. With a schedule I know where I'm supposed to be, but I don't beat myself up when it's not right.

Derek Haas: I give myself an eight-hour writing workday. I usually write new material in the morning, then use the afternoon to polish whatever I worked on that morning. Of course, there's plenty of time thrown in to mess around on the Internet and procrastinate.

Michael Brandt: I like to think I write in the mornings, but usually it happens near the end of the day when the guilt takes over and I feel like I need to jam something out. Guilt is a master motivator.

Jim Kouf: I have several cups of coffee, look at the paper for a little bit, pay some bills, let the caffeine kick in, and then I go at it and try to do it all day.

Andrew W. Marlowe: In my unencumbered life, I'd generally get up, hang out, watch some TV, go to Starbucks, think about stuff all day, and when I finally had an idea, I'd sit down around five in the afternoon and start writing. But now that I'm married and raising kids, I've got to write on a schedule.

Eric Roth: I take my kid to school, come back, take a walk, then I'll jump to the script and start reading from page one, make changes as I go along if I have to, finally get to where the new work starts. By then, I'll have enough momentum to start writing and I'll write for about four hours, and then pick it up again in the evening, where I'll look at what I've done during the day.

Robin Swicord: From the outside, nothing could be duller. I make a cup of tea, I sit down, and I don't move for six hours. I'm usually at my desk by nine and write until four. Sometimes, if the writing is not going well, I'll say to my husband that I'm writing this weekend. This usually means that, either Friday night or Saturday night, I'll be writing until three or four in the morning. This can be good sometimes because it jolts your mind. By varying your routine, you attack the writing when it least expects it.

45. Set Writing Goals

> *Great things are not done by impulse, but by a*
> *series of small things brought together.*
> —Vincent van Gogh

Most professional writers set writing quotas. Whether it's the number of hours of actual writing, number of pages per day, or number of scenes, they produce a given page count on a steady basis. If you make a pact with yourself—reward yourself if you have to—that you won't leave your desk until you've completed a certain number of pages, you'll be surprised at how soon you'll have a completed screenplay.

Leslie Dixon: I try to assign myself a certain amount of pages, and if I do achieve that quota and it's really quite solid, I'll knock off a little early.

Akiva Goldsman: When I'm laying down the first draft, I try to write ten pages a day. Then it's a matter of hours like a regular job. I generally don't write at night and on weekends, because the danger of writing is that you could be doing it anytime. So unless you build rules, you're never free of it.

Andrew W. Marlowe: My daily goal is usually to get to a specific place in the story. But if I don't reach that goal, there can only be two reasons: either I'm mentally fatigued or there's a story problem. Either way, it's good to just walk away, to rest or to let your mind work on that problem. Sometimes it's more effective to just walk away and go work out, play basketball, or have a cup of coffee. Just do something completely different. There's a reason why many people have ideas in the shower—they're relaxed enough to have them.

Bill Marsilii: Once I'm deep into it, five pages a day is a general quota, but that's deceptive because at the beginning of the process, it's like a locomotive trying to leave the station. At first, it's a very slow start, but once it reaches a momentum, it chugs along effortlessly. So at first, it's tough to write even one page, but after a while I get into a white heat and I write morning, day, and night, as well as revising the pages I wrote the day before.

Aline Brosh McKenna: I try to break it down into tasks as much as I can and set goals for the day, like five pages for the day, or edit ten or twenty pages, or do notes. Specific tasks keep me sane.

Terry Rossio: A thousand words a day. Sounds easy, turns out to be impossible.

Tom Schulman: I'm usually very precise at budgeting pages. If I have X number of weeks to finish a project, I'll be very specific as to when

I want to be done and how long I'll give myself on each draft. I try to average twelve pages a day, but it depends on the day, because sometimes I can do twelve pages in two hours. So for me, the goals are more like I want to be done with the first third of it by a certain date, the next third by another date, and so on.

46. Work Even When You're "Not Writing"

*The possibilities of creative effort connected with the
subconscious mind are stupendous and imponderable.
They inspire one with awe.*

—NAPOLEON HILL

Writing doesn't only take place at the keyboard. Just like with Habits 4 (Be a Natural Observer) and 24 (Be Aware of Your Muse's Favorite Activities), you're always observing and your subconscious never takes a break. Though you're not typing, you're still "writing," even when you're sleeping, walking, cooking, playing video games, or just hanging out with your friends.

Derek Haas: Writing is constant, even when I'm not at the desk. I'm always trying to solve the little logic puzzles that'll make the script or novel reach a new level.

Michael Brandt: If I have something that's really troublesome to solve, I'll read the problem area and quit for the day. Usually, lying in bed that night, or in the shower, or some other time when my brain is in idle mode, the answers come.

Amy Holden Jones: Once, when I really got stuck on something, I took a weekend off and went to Santa Barbara. I wasn't thinking about it and woke up in the middle of the night suddenly understanding where I had gone wrong and what I had to change. Sometimes, your mind has to be released in order to get past things, like a muscle that knots up so tight, there isn't enough blood going through it. It has to relax in order for the blood to flow again.

Scott Rosenberg: When you're out in the world, you're observing and hearing people talk. Everyone who knows me and talks to me knows that if I hear a good line, it could wind up in a movie I write.

Terry Rossio: One of the big misconceptions of writing is that it mainly involves putting words down on paper. Certainly that's what producers think. They're forever asking, "Have you started yet?" and "When can we see pages?" But time spent thinking, visualizing, solving story issues, is writing. In fact, that's where the game is won or lost. As William Goldman said, "The hardest thing about writing is knowing what to write." The task of figuring out what to write never stops.

Ed Solomon: When it's going well, you have to drag me away. When it's not, it's hard to stay seated. Sometimes the best way to solve something is to force yourself to actively not write and not think about it. I've come to believe that the subconscious does a great deal of work if you allow it to. I'll actually assign tasks to my subconscious, literally say to myself and type in the computer, "By Monday, figure out X, Y, and Z" and then just leave for the weekend. By Monday, I usually have it figured out.

47. Balance Writing and Personal Life

> *If A equals success, then the formula is A equals X plus Y plus Z. X is work. Y is play. Z is keep your mouth shut.*
> —ALBERT EINSTEIN

One of hardest things for aspiring writers with families or other significant relationships is balancing the pursuit of their dream, which can be all-consuming, with the desire to spend time with their loved ones and the responsibilities of a day job to support them. Too many writers have lost relationships and high-paying jobs because they were too obsessed with making it as a screenwriter.

Though you may think that our mentors have learned to balance their careers and their families because they are now successful, the reality is that, with some exceptions, most had families and relationships when they started out. They just had their priorities straight. In fact, one could argue that knowing what was important grounded them as human beings, which then made them better writers.

Gerald DiPego: I had a regular day job like everyone else. It wasn't easy. It depends on how draining the job is. When I was teaching, I used to get up an hour and a half earlier to write before going to work. With other less mentally taxing jobs, I'd write in the evening.

Derek Haas: At the start of the week, we can see mostly where meetings are going to shake out . . . times when we'll have to be somewhere. Then I can look at the calendar and say, okay, Monday, Tuesday, and Friday are going to be great writing days. I really need to crank some pages on those days because Wednesday and Thursday are shot. I really have to plan it out or all of a sudden, the week went by and I didn't get done what I needed to get done. But I truly love writing, and so it isn't hard for me.

Michael Brandt: I have to block the time out and focus on the task at hand. I love to play golf, so it's easy for me to say, okay, if I play golf this morning, then I have to get back to the office and get this amount of pages done before I quit. It's like a reward for taking some time off.

Amy Holden Jones: I'd work when the kids took naps and after they went to bed. It was an effective motivator because I'd only be able to write about three hours a day, so I wouldn't fool around with doing something else. I just sat down and did it. I think it's harder to write when you have an unlimited amount of time stretching in front of you. But when you have a small window of opportunity, you don't waste it.

Laeta Kalogridis: I have kids. They don't care when it's due. They want you to show up to basketball games and recitals and be on time for dinner and take vacations. They force you to have a life.

Bill Marsilii: I never want to drag my family on my creative roller coaster if I can help it. They're linked to it anyway, but I try to minimize it as much as possible. I never want to reach a point where I'm saying, "Daddy can't come to your concert because he has to write tonight." I do my best to be available to my family. So far, it's worked out pretty well. Since I write in a cottage in my backyard, I'm removed from my house but I'm still home, which is a great balance. And sometimes an interruption from my daughter is exactly what I need when I'm struggling creatively or when I'm having a business frustration.

Aline Brosh McKenna: I take my kids to school. I write from eight-thirty to five-thirty, get home, have dinner with my kids and my husband, and if I need to work I continue working at home.

Michael Schiffer: In the beginning, I tended to overwork and drive myself too hard. When I sold my first book, I was writing around the clock, and a journalist friend of mine said, "You'll kill yourself at this pace. You can't work all day and night. You've got to put it down at six, or decide what your hours are, but write and then stop, and pick it up the next morning. It's a marathon, not a sprint." He convinced me to put a rhythm into my day.

48. Procrastinate

> *Small deeds done are better than great deeds planned.*
> —PETER MARSHALL

Because writing is such an agonizing activity, writers procrastinate in one way or another to alleviate the pressure. They become experts at keeping themselves busy, making excuses—"I'm not in the mood to write," or "There's plenty of time to do it later." While procrastination is often seen as a form of fear (see Habit 38), writers are also told it's an essential step in the creative process: the incubation period. We're supposed to stop writing and do something completely different so that our ideas simmer in our subconscious, ready to flash great ideas at any moment. So procrastination is acceptable if it only takes a small chunk out of your available writing time. But if it prevents you from finishing a script, it may be a negative habit. The difference between pros and amateurs is that the pros control how long they procrastinate.

Steven de Souza: I know I'm about to write when I become a neat-freak and start rearranging the pens and pencils around, noodling things in my brain, and basically wasting time until I get that caffeine rush.

Leslie Dixon: I call them "stalling mechanisms." We all have them. Writers who are close friends will be honest with each other; they'll say, "Okay, I'm avoiding work," and next thing you know, you have a forty-five-minute conversation. You waste time by checking your e-mail when you get up, drinking your coffee, or reading the paper. I guess you over-come that by feeling guilty and yelling at yourself to get on with it. In some cases, it's "Don't you want to get rid of this project? Aren't these people horrible? Don't you want to turn this in as soon as possible so you can go on to something else? Write!!" Procrastination can actually be a very interesting tool for success, because if you can control it, you have a leg up on the competition. If you're known as a person who can produce quality work in a reasonable period of time, they'll be much quicker to hire you over the writer who takes a year to write a script.

Tony Gilroy: I hate the idea of just sitting around and nothing hap-pening, spinning my wheels and going nowhere. I want to make myself want to be there at the desk. The whole goal is to try to create a situation where it's either too painful not to be there, where I'm so afraid that everything will just disappear if I'm not there. So it's all a mental game to make myself want to be there—where I really want to wake up and get to the keyboard, where I'm hurrying up to get back from lunch because I love a particular sequence and I can't think of anything else.

There's all kinds of games where you try to get yourself to con-tinue, like "I need money to pay the rent," or "These people are really assholes, I'm gonna show them," or "If I don't make my deadline, I won't be able to go away and be with my family." You write from anger, you write from fear, but mostly you write from excitement—"This is so cool, I can't wait to show this to somebody."

Terry Rossio: My best motivator is the paycheck. Not really the desire for it, but the enormous guilt that arrives with it. A check, or a contract for a check, is a huge act of faith on the part of someone.

Procrastination hurts only myself, and that's fine, I'll do that all year long. But when it's going to hurt someone else, that's where it gets unacceptable.

49. Make Deadlines Your Motivator

> *I shall meet all of my deadlines directly in proportion to the amount of bodily injury I could expect to receive from missing them.*
> —Procrastinator's Creed

For a professional screenwriter, nothing beats a deadline to get scripts finished. But just because you don't have a contract and due date for your spec doesn't mean you can't create self-imposed deadlines for your project. The problem is that they're not as powerful, since you're only accountable to yourself.

So the most effective deadlines are the ones involving other people, either writers in a group, where pages are expected weekly, or friends who will penalize you if you don't submit a finished draft on time. When you're accountable to someone else, you'll have no choice but to finish that draft. As the saying goes, "Nothing makes a person more productive than the last minute."

Steven de Souza: Deadlines are the greatest motivator I know; how could they not be? They're the reason I got my quota of six pages out of it. I realized I needed to write X number of pages by a certain time and I divided that by the number of days. The calendar is my best friend.

Derek Haas: If I ever try to set page goals, I end up falling short or quitting before I'm ready because, well, I made my goal. So I just look at it the way Brandt does—I'm going to finish this script by a certain date. It's all about deadlines. You know that you'll want to get favorable reads from the studio execs and you don't want them sitting down pissed off because it took forever to get the first draft. So you try to hit those deadlines.

Michael Brandt: No page quotas for me. I write until it's not good anymore, or I run out of time. I rarely run out of time.

Andrew W. Marlowe: When I had a day job, it was putting aside three or four hours a night to write and giving myself deadlines, because without a deadline, without making a commitment, either to yourself or to someone else that you'll deliver finished pages by a particular date, things can drift for a very long time. When I didn't have the financially imposed deadlines of studio executives waiting for it, I belonged to a writer's group that met once a week. This meant that during the week I had to write fifteen pages so that we could talk about them. This forced to me to actually fulfill that commitment or risk showing up empty-handed and embarrass myself. Knowing that human beings procrastinate, knowing that there was no obligation for me to write, I had to create one to force discipline on myself.

Bill Marsilii: Obviously they're crucial when you've been paid and there's a contract. You're truly accountable then. It's harder when you're writing on spec because you're only accountable to yourself, so it's easy for things to drag out indefinitely. Not only does a deadline help to get things finished, it also helps creatively, because the muse wouldn't bother getting out of bed if it didn't have somewhere to be in twelve weeks. Being in love with your story also helps. You want to see the movie so bad that you just can't wait to finish it.

Scott Rosenberg: My goal is to finish a script, so it's not a matter of pages or hours, but more about a deadline. I won't allow myself to spend more than two or three months on a given script.

CHAPTER 10

WRITER'S BLOCK

50. Combat Writer's Block

> *If you're going to be a writer, the first essential is just to
> write. Do not wait for an idea. Start writing something
> and the ideas will come. You have to turn the faucet on
> before the water starts to flow.*
>
> —Louis L'Amour

If you're writing regularly, sometimes the well runs dry. No words or
images come to mind. Some writers panic at the first sign of block
and rush to their shrinks, while others believe it's only a temporary
setback and have a bag of tricks to overcome it, like taking a shower,
driving, exercising, or writing in a journal to vent their frustrations on
the page.

Many writers like to revise pages they've already written, which
inspires them to write more. Others follow Hemingway's favorite trick:
stopping in the middle of a scene, leaving it incomplete, knowing
exactly how to end it. This way they start the day looking forward to
finishing the scene.

Sometimes, writers are blocked because they're just not ready yet.
Maybe more research is needed, or the story needs to mature through
incubation. So they embrace it as part of the creative process, letting
it marinate without feeling the guilt of being unproductive, and knowing that what they don't write is as important as what they do write.

Michael Brandt: If I get stuck, I can just pass it over to Derek or he can do the same to me. I highly suggest having a partner if you can find one who shares your same voice.

Gerald DiPego: Certainly, there are slow days, where your mind feels like it's made of honey. If I can't seem to tap into the right creative energy, I'll sometimes walk away. Sometimes, I'll use specific tricks. For example, if a scene isn't working, I'll shake things up by changing the setting completely, or I'll change one important element in the scene, and see what happens. But when something isn't working, it's usually because I'm rushing it. Either I'm not taking the time to stay with the core of the reality of the story, or I haven't individualized the characters enough and I've started writing these characters before fleshing them out completely.

Leslie Dixon: I've only had it once and it was absolutely horrible. It lasted two weeks and the reason was that I thought it was going to be an easy adaptation of a novel that just read like a dream. When I got into it, I realized I had to make big changes in order to turn it into a movie. I was in such despair that I almost gave the money back and said I can't do it. This was a job I really wanted and felt really passionate about, and I felt like a worthless idiot. So I called this shrink I go to once in a while, and said, "I never really experienced this before. Is writer's block a real thing? How long is it supposed to last?" And he said, "Between two and five weeks, don't worry about it." He just gave me this very specific answer, it was hilarious. Somehow, it gave my subconscious permission to provide me with the solution.

Tony Gilroy: I often deal with it, not in the sense that I can't write, but of not knowing what I want to say thematically, or not finding what's interesting about the moment. That's the most painful thing, a sort of self-induced bipolar depression when it's not working. I'd hate to think of the amount of hours, days, and months that I'd just sit there getting nothing done. So I constantly try to find what's interesting and new and fresh, something that hasn't been done before. It's always about getting excited about *what* you're writing, what's *worth* putting on the page. That's the tough part.

Nicholas Kazan: I believe it exists but I've never had any difficulty writing. I believe it was B. F. Skinner, of all people, who said that if he deserved any credit, it was for being at a location where certain processes could take place. As a writer, if you're doing your job well, you're placing your talent at a place where it can be worked by creative forces. I know it sounds mystical, but it's basically about putting yourself in a situation where you can tap into the forces of society and humanity, that collective unconscious, and write things that come out of yourself, relatively unguided and uncensored. Sometimes the writing is better than at other times. It's okay to say, "I just don't have it today." But this usually happens in the early stages when I'm writing notes and I don't feel connected to it.

Aline Brosh McKenna: In a strange way, I feel it's *all* writer's block. I think your brain would rather sit on the couch and read the newspaper or watch TV. It's all about saying, "I'm going to sit there and I'm going to write, but it's hard." What worked for me in the beginning was to set small, concrete goals, like sit there for an hour and just force myself to do it.

Ed Solomon: I don't often suffer from [writer's block]. I suffer from the opposite: too many things I want to write. But I know it exists for people. It also depends on whether you're talking about a chronic thing, or if you're just having trouble with a particular scene for a couple of days. One useful trick for me is to sit down and write about the problem I'm having. I'll literally write, "Okay, now I'm going to try to figure out why I cannot solve this problem. When I figure out how to do this," etcetera. Actually writing about the problem often unlocks things for me and leads me to a whole new series of ideas. Another trick is to actively not write and trust your subconscious to work on it. That doesn't mean blow it off.

51. Don't Believe in Writer's Block

> *Writer's block is a fancy term made up by whiners*
> *so they can have an excuse to drink alcohol.*
> —STEVE MARTIN

Some writers believe writer's block doesn't exist. It's just another word for fear—fear of failure, of being exposed as a fraud, or feeling your writing isn't good enough. This statement alone should help open your creative floodgates on days they'd rather be closed. The bottom line is there will be days when the words flow and days when they don't. On the days they do, you're happy to write. On the days they don't, you write anyway, even if you're not happy about it. The only trick is to get something on paper. You can always edit it later. When you adopt this attitude, block is no longer some evil, mystical phenomenon that paralyzes you for months.

Steven de Souza: I never have writer's block. Not because I don't hit the wall like everyone else, but because whenever I get stuck in a scene, I just jump to another part of the movie. There's always another scene you can write today if you're stuck elsewhere. I always write what's clearest in my mind.

I'd call it a "roadblock," not writer's block. What do you do when you hit a roadblock? You take an alternate route. You don't just wait there until they finish the roadwork so you can drive through.

Akiva Goldsman: Sure, I've had day upon day where I couldn't write anything particularly good, but you just write through it. Just write bad stuff.

Jim Kouf: I never had the situation where you just stare at the screen and nothing happens. Sometimes, I know what I'm thinking maybe isn't the best idea, but this usually leads me to something better, so I've never been completely empty. For me, it's like being on a jungle path. If there's a lot of stuff in your way, you hack through it. You don't whine, "Oh, it's too thick." You pick up the machete and chop.

Andrew W. Marlowe: I got over the fear of the blank page when I learned that it's okay to write shitty stuff, which is the portal to writing the good stuff. So when you think of it, there's no such thing as "writer's block." There's simply "writer's embarrassment" because anybody can put words on the page. You're physically capable of putting words on the page. You just don't want to because you know they're shitty. You're embarrassed by them. But if you can get over that embarrassment and give yourself permission to write absolute crap, generally by the third or fourth page, stuff becomes good or you find something meaningful. Give yourself permission to write poorly before you can write well.

Eric Roth: I've never had it, but I believe other writers can get frozen. I think, in a way, it's about having the courage to fail. If you have no fear of failure, what's the difference? You have to force yourself to write through it, otherwise you'll never end it. So if a scene bothers you, just sort of sketch it in, blow past it and then come back to it later. You might find you never needed it at all. If I get stuck on a difficult scene, I'll sometimes change the weather. For instance, if it's raining, it will open up a whole new world. Or maybe I'll realize I went down the wrong road, so I'll back up and go down a different road.

52. Write Terrible First Drafts

> *My best writing is done by writing rapidly and with*
> *few filters. I then delete my way to excellence.*
> —RICHARD BACH

Most professional screenwriters have become comfortable with writing a lot of bad stuff in order to come up with a little good stuff. They often produce thousands of words before one line is fresh enough to jump off the page. To do this, they give themselves permission to write anything, no matter how terrible, because they know it can all be fixed later, thus giving them the power to free themselves sufficiently in the creative stage to write from the heart while silencing their inner critic.

Steven de Souza: I like writing the first draft, which I blaze through as fast as I can, without even stopping for spell- or fact-checking that might interrupt the flow. And I like the editing part of the printed first draft with my trusty red pen, though I hate all the retyping from the edited page into the computer. On the other hand, I never get depressed about what I write, because I know I'm going to rewrite it. I remember seeing an interview with George Lucas where he talks about a trick he learned from Francis Coppola, which is not to read what he's writing until he's done with it. He writes nonstop, puts the pages in a file, and it's not until he thinks he's done with it that he'll find the nerve to look at his pages.

Jim Kouf: You just write, blindly putting things down on paper. Just put something down, and then put something else down, because it's a process of thinking through all the choices. You have to be willing to throw it away. If you write something awful, you just say, "Okay, I tried," and sometimes you make it all the way through to discover it's not worth it. You've got to write. Don't be afraid to make mistakes.

Tom Schulman: Silencing that inner critic is important, at least through the first draft, because when will you have another chance to let it all out, if not in the first draft? I try to finish the first draft before rewriting it, and ultimately, I'll go over it about ten to twelve times. But I usually go over the first third of the script and rewrite it until it's good enough because I feel that if it's launched properly, the rest will follow through.

CHAPTER 11

REWRITING

53. Finish Your Draft Before Rewriting

Compose first, worry later.
—NED ROREM

Finishing what you write before editing it has a double benefit. It prevents you from tinkering with it too much, which could be a dangerous form of procrastination. Too many writers, sometimes laboring over the same opening ten pages for years, take forever to finish their script. The other benefit is that it allows you to step away from it for a period of time, anywhere from one week to a month, so that you may come back to it with a fresh pair of eyes, able to look at it as objectively as possible.

Akiva Goldsman: I try to build the story as cleanly as I can, make sure the structure works, then I write it really badly, as fast as I can, ten pages a day of shit, sometimes actual dialogue, sometimes notes to myself about what people will say in the scene, just to get some feeling of the shape of the piece, trying not to rewrite it, unless I'm feeling I'm so cheating myself. Then I go back and start rewriting. And I go over and over and over it, scene by scene, then act by act, then sequence by sequence, until it's as tight and clean as I can possibly make it.

Derek Haas: I usually write an entire first pass that is truly a "vomit" draft. I don't care about the characters making sense, or the theme coming through, or the subtext working. I basically just get the plot down into 110 pages. Then we get notes and meet and Michael comes in with a wrecking ball and the script really starts to take shape. From there, we pass it back and forth twenty times until we're satisfied with the draft. At this point, I usually can't tell what I wrote and what he wrote. It truly is a great collaboration.

Laeta Kalogridis: Draft, notes, then rewrite. Rinse and repeat.

Jim Kouf: The number of drafts depends on whether I'm happy with it. Usually I write about 75 percent of it and then go back and start looking at it. Sometimes, I write the whole script before looking at it and going through every word again and again. Sometimes you have to set it down for a while and get away from it. If I feel happy with it, I give it to my wife, and if she's happy with it, I give it to my agents, and if they like it, we do something with it.

Aline Brosh McKenna: I write out of sequence. I just write scenes, go forward and backwards all over the script. I try to write as many pages as I can before I start rewriting. Once you start rewriting, you get in the weeds, so I like to get a sense of the whole before I start rewriting.

Scott Rosenberg: I'm all for dumping it out first and coming back to it.

54. Rewrite as You Go Along

It's like driving a car at night. You never see further than your headlights, but you can make the whole trip that way.
— E. L. Doctorow

Some screenwriters work differently, though. They don't go forward until they feel a particular page or scene is good enough.

Leslie Dixon: You often know when you're not hitting it, so I generally rewrite as I go along. But often, it's in your best interest to forget about it and get a certain volume of pages. I usually go back to the first thirty pages a number of times. If I get it to where it's pretty good, that gives me steam to go all the way to the end without stopping again.

Tony Gilroy: I'm constantly rewriting as I go along. Writing, printing it out, editing it, changing it on the computer. Constantly.

Amy Holden Jones: I'm afraid to write terrible first drafts but I still write them, rewriting incessantly almost every day from page one. When I can make myself not do this, I'll try to write twenty pages at a time without going back.

Andrew W. Marlowe: I'm a firm believer that you get stuff out and you start shaping it, that whatever you put on the page is like clay that you then sculpt. But I like to finish long chunks of stuff before I start reshaping. I'll write fifteen or so pages without my internal editor, then I'll go back and shape those, just so that I know where I'm going next. But I don't try to make these pages perfect because I think that perfection is the enemy of completion. That said, if I'm writing unedited for too long, I could lose specificity and I become very broad and unfocused as I get toward the end of the story.

Bill Marsilii: My morning and early afternoons are spent revising what I did the night before. Which means that by the time I'm done with the first draft, each scene has been rewritten two or three times. I know writers who like to write a first draft as quickly as possible and then go back to it to revise, referring to it as their "vomit" draft. I'd never use that horrible word. If you must, call it your "brainstorm" draft. My feeling is that if you start with vomit, you'll never get all the stench out, no matter how many times you rework it. Leonardo da Vinci did not start the *Mona Lisa* by slopping paint all over the canvas just to get something down, thinking, "I'll smooth it out later."

Eric Roth: I go back to page one every single day. I keep refining and refining as I go through it. Sometimes I'll let things go in the first draft that I'll later come back to, because when you get enough experience, you know what will make or break a piece.

Ed Solomon: The difference between a professional and a beginner is that while they both write a lot of crap, the pro knows when to show it and when not to. It's just about editing more effectively. In theory, my method is to go all the way through a first draft and then rewrite. But in reality, I tend to look at it the next day. One way I avoid this is by creating files that are only fifteen to twenty pages long. Once I reach twenty pages of a script, I close that file and start a new one. This way I go over a script in twenty-page chunks. And I resist, as much as possible, the tendency to continue rehashing the first half of the movie.

55. Make the Script as Good as It Can Be

Only a mediocre writer is always at his best.
—W. Somerset Maugham

Often, the biggest mistake beginners make is submitting a script too soon, usually a first draft. They're too impatient, desperate for something to happen, because they've been at it for so long. Maybe they think the script is good enough because it's better than the latest Hollywood flop they've just seen at the multiplex. Or, the most common phenomenon: they think it's good just because the script is finally *done*. Big mistake. All they've done is burn a bridge to that one connection who was willing to read their script. In this town, you only get one chance to shine. By sending an inferior script, they've only guaranteed that that producer, agent, or assistant will never read anything from them again. Even when professional writers feel they've done their best, they still get a second opinion. As Maxwell Perkins once said, "If you are not discouraged about your writing on a regular basis, you may not be trying hard enough."

Leslie Dixon: Being a tough self-critic is a hugely important thing. If you can see your work with a laser eye, you're in a much better position, because if you can police your own work, rather than wait for somebody else to tell you what's wrong with it, you can be part of the process of how your script changes and therefore have more control about what happens to your work. Too many writers wait to be told what's wrong with their scripts.

Tony Gilroy: Be hard on yourself before anyone else. It always astonishes me how many writers just want to be told how great their writing is. If you give them a note like, "This is a good idea, but your third act is really the beginning of a movie, you should really explore it," their answer is, "Do you know how long I've been working on this?!" Anybody who has a moment's hesitation about throwing away anything that doesn't work, no matter how hard it was to acquire, is fooling themselves.

It also astounds me that writers who have seen thousands and thousands of movies write something that doesn't even look like a movie. You're writing a movie. You have a movie in your head and you try to describe it as best you can. When you're reading a script, you can tell whether the writer can see the movie or not. If you can't see the movie, it's worthless.

Bill Marsilii: Be better and more diligent than everyone else. Don't settle for first draft theatre. Don't settle for being "good enough." Far too many writers read screenwriting primers and think, "Something interesting has to happen on page thirty and on page ninety. That should be easy." No, how about something interesting happening on every page, every line? And don't get me started on typos. I've never read a good script that was full of typos. Typos are the kind of sloppiness that typically extends to every other part of the process. If you're careless about your work, chances are you're careless about the craft.

Terry Rossio: Since I'm essentially an editor at heart, I'm constantly rewriting and polishing. Nothing ever gets turned it that hasn't been rewritten at least forty times, or more.

56. Get Feedback

> *Ask advice from everyone, but act with your own mind.*
> —Yiddish proverb

There's a popular joke among Hollywood executives: "How many screenwriters does it take to change a light bulb?"

"Oh, no! Not the light bulb!"

All writers can relate. They don't like changing anything because it's their sweat, blood, and soul on the page. But you have to be objective about your work to improve it. If you're serious about becoming a successful screenwriter, you have to see the story from a reader's perspective before it's read by someone important. This requires unbiased feedback, preferably from experienced writers or story analysts.

Michael Brandt: [Derek and I] get feedback from each other, and then our manager reads every draft of everything we write. He gives excellent notes and really is a creative partner on our drafts.

Steven de Souza: I'd definitely recommend writers get good feedback on their material. I get a lot of writers who give me their script and say, "Here's my movie. I know you'll like it and I'd really like your notes because you're the best at doing action movies. The first act is a little long and the plot needs some work and I'm not sure if the hero's buddy should be a guy or a girl, but here, read it." Now, if you know these things are wrong with this draft, don't give it to me now.

And half the time they say, "No, no, I really want your notes so I can incorporate them into my next version," and I say, "I'm only going to read this once. You only get one shot. You have to make this as good as you can get it before you give it to me. Now go away."

Gerald DiPego: When I'm writing something, whether it's a script or a novel, my wife enjoys it when I read the day's work to her in the evening after dinner. It really helps me because I can hear it out loud, look at it again, and observe her reaction. She's the perfect audience because she loves film but she's not a student of it.

Once I get a first draft, I give it to my two sons, who are also screenwriters, and who give me valuable feedback. Not only do they know the craft but they also represent the younger generation. So between my wife and my two sons, I feel very lucky to get valuable feedback.

Leslie Dixon: I don't have that many dead-ass, reliable sources for feedback except for my husband, and occasionally my agent. I also have a couple of writer friends with whom I occasionally trade scripts.

But I go more by my own gut than anything. I just try to please myself. Do I like this script? Would I pay eleven dollars to see this? These are pretty big questions if you're honest with yourself.

Akiva Goldsman: I usually let a couple of trusted readers read it. Usually, they should not be friends or family, but they can be if you trust them to tell you what you wrote sucks, because better they say it sucks than Steven Spielberg saying it. Then when you're at a place where you're okay with it, you let the world take a look.

Laeta Kalogridis: I try to make sure I have different people reading each draft so I have at least one set of fresh eyes each time.

Nicholas Kazan: When I finish a script, I show it to between two and ten people before turning it in. I have a couple of criteria on the feedback. If one person says something, and I don't agree with it, I ignore it. If two people say it, then I start to worry. If three people say it, I have a real problem, whether I like it or not, and I have to do something. If I think it's a good idea conceptually, but I don't know how to do it, I don't worry about it. There are always ideas for a more brilliant version of any script, but it may not be the movie I want to write, or that I'm capable of writing.

Tom Schulman: I have three people I show everything to. They're not writers, but I trust them because they always tell me everything. Sometimes, they can't articulate what's right or wrong with something, but I can tell by this sort of lack of response to a scene I thought was particularly good, or their enthusiasm for something I thought was particularly weak. I also find it necessary to ask a lot of questions, like: "Did you like this character? Are you really pulling for him here? What do you think this character wants out of life?" People often don't bring things up unless you ask them.

Ed Solomon: I try not to show a script in its early stages to highly critical people because they might kill it. Who you give the script to is a very important decision to make, especially when you're starting out. People who are available to you at your level are also young and vulnerable and have their own ego and self-image at stake. They often can be well-intentioned on one level, but on a deeper level they can be destructive in ways that don't necessarily seem destructive. You need to be very careful about what you take to heart. Be very skeptical about people's solutions to your script's problems.

57. Be Open to Outside Criticism

Don't mind criticism. If it's untrue, disregard it.
If it's unfair, keep from irritation. If it's ignorant, smile.
If it's justified, learn from it.
—OLD CHINESE SAYING

When faced with feedback on a script, no writer with an ounce of sensitivity wants to be told what's wrong with it. It's easy to feel hurt and defensive, and hard not to take even constructive criticism personally. This is why it's so difficult getting honest feedback from friends and family. They know how vulnerable we are.

One habit professionals have, though, is being willing to listen to criticism and not react defensively to it. Instead of arguing over every note, take it all in and think about it. As the writer, you're in complete control to accept or reject the notes, but the only surefire way to improve is to understand when what you're doing isn't working.

Michael Brandt: After we get our manager's notes, we sit down and have a "cigar session" where we talk out what the next pass is going to be. We don't get defensive about what we wrote. The best idea wins on the rewrite.

Nicholas Kazan: There's no such thing as constructive criticism. All criticism is destructive because it's felt by the author as destructive. All criticism says is (a) you didn't do this part well, and (b) there's something wrong with you. At least, that's how it's experienced. You want to kill your critics, but you need to listen.

Recently I've been taking my laptop computer to story meetings, and it's been very helpful because whatever pain I feel, it just moves through my fingers and down into the computer. I'm just typing away whatever they're saying. Then, I go home and think about it, and often it's not as bad as my first impression. When you listen and analyze the problem, solutions present themselves.

Andrew W. Marlowe: The way I look at it is that my audience is reading the script and watching the movie in their minds. Are they responding the way I want them to respond? Because all writing is emotional manipulation. So if they aren't responding the way I want them to, I can't argue with that and tell them that they're wrong to feel that way. So I have to ask them, "Okay, this is not how I wanted you to feel. What's missing? Is there something that I have in my head that I didn't put on the page?" When I read it, I know all this stuff because it's in my head, but have I communicated that to the reader? If they say they weren't heartbroken in that scene, I ask them why, what's missing for them? Never ask those questions from the point of view of ego, of being personally attacked, but from the view that it's a story and it can get better. Knowing what works and what doesn't emotionally for the reader will help in making the story better.

Bill Marsilii: Notes tend to fall into three categories: good, lateral, or damaging. The good notes are the ones that improve the script, and you should be thankful for those. The lateral notes are the ones that don't affect any major points. Someone might prefer a character's hair to be blonde instead of brunette. Sure, no problem. These can be implemented painlessly and aren't worth debating. And then you have the damaging notes. Those you need to be diligent about. The phrase "Pick your battles" comes up a lot for these. The degree to which you've been accommodating on the other notes will earn you some degree of stature where you can discuss these notes, and say, for instance, "I have a problem with that one, and let me tell you what we will gain or lose if we make this change here." It's not about saying no. More like, "Here's my concern if we do this." Ideally you want them to hear you out, and have *them* say, "Never mind, ignore that note." And if you can also offer another solution that addresses their concern, so much the better. At times like that, I try to listen to the first half of the note, where they describe the symptom, what they think is wrong. Their proposed way to fix that problem is often mistaken, but that doesn't mean one should disregard the entire note. Always remember that all they're trying to do is improve the script, so it should be an amicable process, not open warfare.

Robin Swicord: What's good about giving your script to more than one person is that in the end, the notes are not so personal. If I give it to a few people, someone will like something. The most important thing is that if you hear something once, they could be wrong, but if you hear the same problem more than once, you have to pay attention. Notes are symptomatic, so you have to be good at hearing them in such a way that you can interpret these notes, and don't rush the process when there might be another solution.

● ● ●

Discipline is critical, but like a tree that doesn't make a sound if no one is there to hear it fall, a screenwriter without a great script won't get any attention in Hollywood. What makes a great script? Art and craft. Art is your talent. No one can "teach" it to you. But let's find out what our mentors have to say about craft.

PART 4

STORYCRAFT

Weaving a Great Tale

*Nothing counts as much as the story, because it's
the story that will attract the director, the actors,
the studio, the money. The story is the thing.*
—DAVID BROWN

CHAPTER 12

WHAT MAKES A GREAT SCRIPT

58. Discriminate Between Good and Bad Writing

*The most essential gift for a good writer is a
built-in, shock-proof shit detector.*
—ERNEST HEMINGWAY

A prerequisite for success as a screenwriter is the ability to tell the
difference between good and bad writing before anyone of importance (the buyer) finds out for himself. Professionals say that if the
writing moves them in any way, if they identify with the characters,
are involved in the story, and experience surprises and emotional satisfaction, it's good. If it's unoriginal, clichéd, and boring, it's bad. To
develop this skill of discernment, it helps to read as many screenplays
as possible, not only classic ones to aspire to excellence, but terrible
ones as well to avoid making the same mistakes.

Steven de Souza: I'm guilty of what many executives do, which is
to give scripts ten pages to hold my interest. I can be enthralled by
a historical drama—or even (*gasp!*) a chick flick—if it's well written.
Sometimes, I'll just read the dialogue, then alternatively only the stage
directions. Ideally, one without the other should not be able to get the
story across. So a good test of dialogue is to just read the dialogue for
a section of the script. If that leaves you hungry for more, that's good.
But if I get the entire story with just the dialogue, then all that stage
direction is just dead weight and useless.

Akiva Goldsman: You just know what's good or bad. There's no answer to this, and you're not always right. I was asked once by an interviewer why I wrote a particular line that was terrible. And I said I wrote it in the same way I wrote all the lines he thought were good. It's not like you sit there and go, "Now let's write some really bad lines."

Making a movie is like painting a mural on the side of a wall at night, and your only light is a lightning storm. So there are flashes of light, and we're sort of painting really quickly, gradually doing the whole thing, and then morning comes and we get to see what we've done, and we either go, "Wow, that's great," or "God, what did I just do?"

There are a few things first-time writers do that they could avoid. They don't really study the form, both in terms of structure and what it looks like on the page. There are definite formatting conventions that for some strange reason are often ignored by first-timers. You open up a script and see six giant paragraphs of text, or the dialogue goes all the way to the right, or there are way too many camera directions, and you can tell you're dealing with a beginner. Also, misspelled words blow me away, especially in this age of spell-checkers. All these mistakes are a sign of laziness, so you should be smart about it. Then, people try to write what they think screenplays sound like, rather than writing the way people talk, and really listening to what people say. I do have a pretty good ear for dialogue. I sort of know what people sound like. I can look at a sentence and see its rhythms. Some of it is learned, a lot of it comes from reading and listening, and a little bit comes from the right set of chromosomes.

Amy Holden Jones: I can usually tell on the first page. Believe it or not, many people use bad grammar, and they're too lazy to correct it. They also don't understand that people who read a lot of scripts don't want to read elaborate descriptions, especially if it's in bad grammar. There's a certain quality in the dialogue, without straining to be literary, that tells you whether it's written by a writer or not. It's the kind of writing that pulls you in and just makes you want to know what happens next.

Nicholas Kazan: Good writing is usually idiosyncratic. The writing feels like a movie, rather than a screenplay. There's a specificity of detail and a sense of command. It's like when you're sitting around the campfire. One person really knows how to tell a story, and when it begins, you say, "This is going to be good!" When you read a screenplay, you want that same sense of anticipation. You don't know where it's going, but you know from the first page that it will be good.

Jim Kouf: You know bad writing when you read it. The dialogue is not sharp, the characters are not as interesting or as funny or as charming as they should be, the story is not as clever as it can be. Ultimately, good writing can't be boring. You've got to be clever. Why are we going to sit through it for two hours?

Scott Rosenberg: You can tell from the first page if someone can write, by its assuredness and its confidence. What this does is allow you to relax immediately and say, "Okay, you can write, now tell me a story." If, right off the bat, there are four-inch blocks of text, or it's not formatted properly, you know it's an amateur.

Eric Roth: The one thing I notice about bad scripts is that there's too much exposition. People talk too much and tell you what you've already seen. It's just tedious writing, telling you things instead of showing. I'm a very visual writer, so some of the exposition I write is just in the visual. Subtext is very important. It's always terrific to write about something else and still tell the audience what's really going on.

Michael Schiffer: The first thing you listen for is whether the words move you in some way. The language itself speaks to you. As a writer, you hope that your words generate a feeling of excitement, and in a crazy way, that maybe there's something there. Initially, reality testing may tell you otherwise. But what you're looking for is that spark, hoping that others will see it too.

Tom Schulman: It's the old Harry Cohn thing: You know a good script by how much you're squirming in your seat. The producer who hired me to write my first script also hired me to read scripts. For about four months, I was reading about five scripts a day. When you pick up a script, you start by being optimistic; you want to believe this will be a great script. But within a few pages, it either grabs you and sucks you in, or you find yourself having to just push and push into it. If by page thirty you have to fight to stay awake, there's something wrong. Sure, something great could happen on page forty, but it's too late. Today's executives usually don't give you more than five or ten pages.

Ed Solomon: A script is good if I get emotionally involved. You can usually tell if it's bad writing when it doesn't affect you in any way. Also, I find a singular or interesting voice far more affecting and inspiring than a "perfectly" plotted or structured piece.

59. Understand It Takes Talent and Hard Work

> *A writer is a person for whom writing is more*
> *difficult than it is for other people.*
> —Thomas Mann

The most common and erroneous belief among nonprofessional writers is that writing a movie is no harder than watching one, and that because movies and TV shows are plentiful, relatively short, and frequently mediocre, there really are few rules, standards, or professional skills to worry about. In other words, screenwriting is easy.

When asked why there are so many (the accepted percentage is 99 percent) bad scripts out there, our mentors responded that writing requires both talent and hard work.

Ron Bass: For some reason, there's a notion that writing is something anyone could do. Because everybody owns a computer and everybody knows the English language and likes to go to the movies or read books and think about stories, everybody thinks they could do it. The key is: Can everybody not only do it well but do it well enough that you'd want to pay money to go see that story? We all drive cars, but how many of us could drive at Indianapolis? Every woman in the world puts on makeup, but how many could become a runway model in Milan? Nobody can stop you from putting on makeup. You just never get to the runway, because someone has to *ask* you to model their clothes. It's the same with the desire to become a screenwriter. You don't need anyone's permission. It doesn't cost you anything. All you have to do is write 110 pages and print them. It's kind of a blessing in a sense, because nobody can stop you. So if it's your goal, why not give it a try? Starting is easy; making it is another story. There's a certain ability needed to do anything, be it natural talent, intelligence, passion, desire, experience, whatever it is that makes people good at anything that needs to be done at a high enough level for other people to want to support it. When you get down to somebody spending $80 million to make a movie out of a script, do we really think *anyone* could do it?

Leslie Dixon: The only reason most scripts are bad is because most people can't write. Look at all the things you have to do to be a screenwriter. You have to be able to tell a good story. Most people can't do that. They haven't even read the great literature of all time, or seen the great films of all time, to see how it should be done. So where are they going to learn what a basic good yarn is? Because this is your first obligation as a screenwriter. You need some contact with your soul to create rich, interesting characters, and writing talent to make them jump off the page. You need to have an ear for human speech, and you need to entertain the reader in a way that keeps him moving pages. Right away, this is a lot to ask.

Akiva Goldsman: Unfortunately, people believe that their first thing should be great. Writing is like anything else. You're not supposed to write a page and expect it to be good. You have to write a thousand bad pages to get to that one good page. It's as if we were training for the twenty-yard dash, and instead of waiting until we'd trained before we ran, we invite everyone to our first practice, and, of course, we fall flat on our face.

Amy Holden Jones: People don't know what they want to say and don't spend enough time learning how to say it. Too many try to write screenplays without doing the hard work. They have the mentality that it's easy, and the reality is that it's probably one of the hardest things they'll ever do. First, you need a strong commercial instinct. Many wonderful writers I know have failed because they didn't have this commercial instinct or were unable to deal with the collaborative nature of the medium. Many scripts would be better if writers were very disciplined, if they did the necessary research, and if they had some sort of sensitivity toward people in the way they really behave and talk to each other. Another reason why scripts fail is that the lead character's need, motivation, or goal is often not clear. You have to know what they want, no matter what it is or how goofy it is. And if you don't care about what they want, you won't be emotionally invested in the character.

Scott Rosenberg: It's purely a numbers thing. Anyone can write screenplays in the privacy of their own home. An actor needs lines and a director needs a blueprint. And we all go to movies and we're always disappointed in them. We walk out saying, "They should have done this and that." So basically, everyone with a computer can write a screenplay, and everyone does, despite the fact that they may not be qualified.

I sometimes go to these seminars and see people who have paid thousands of dollars, and they all know each other, and they go to every seminar because they think we hold some magic pill, and you read some of their stuff and it's like, "My God! My grandmother on her worst day, who's never written a single word in her life, could write better than this." The level of windmills they're tilting at is enormous. Will they ever make it? Probably not. But if it makes them happy to do it, you can't blame them.

Eric Roth: I think people don't spend the amount of time necessary to rewrite a script and all the detailed work you need to really understand the characters.

Michael Schiffer: Hollywood is full of people who want to make easy money the hard way. People see a bad movie and say, "I can do that." Writing is incredibly hard, and most people trying to do it don't believe this is true. They're not working as hard as the task requires, and it shows on the pages. Since you don't break in by being bad, the question should be, "How do I get really good? How do I reach this level where my work is so unmistakably excellent that nobody can read it and not be impressed?"

People ask me all the time how to break in. I honestly believe that if you get your work to the point where your writing speaks for itself, where it's categorically and objectively terrific and it moves the reader, you'll get noticed. Readers will sit up and say, "Wow, that was well written." They may not want to buy the movie, but they'll definitely want to be in business with you.

Tom Schulman: Too many aspiring writers push their first work too early. Dan Petrie Jr. once said that to become a doctor takes four years of medical school and four years of internship and residency, and to be a lawyer takes three years of law school plus so many years to work yourself up through the firm. Most people assume writing screenplays is something they can do in a couple of afternoons.

The reality is that in order to be good at it, it will probably take you as long as any other profession to master the craft. So it's possible that this 99 percent of bad material we read comes from people who just haven't put in the time and effort, and it's their first or second script. Of course, there's always someone who can write a great screenplay right off the bat, but it's this 1 percent exception.

60. Trust Your Instincts

*Don't write what you know—what you know
may bore you, and thus bore your readers.
Write about what interests you—and interests you deeply—
and your readers will catch fire at your words.*
—Valerie Sherwood

Write what excites you and never second-guess your instincts. The common advice is to write what you know, but it should be to write what makes you *feel*, what intrigues and fascinates you, because ultimately, the only thing you really know are your emotions. After all, doesn't everyone *feel* in the same language?

As William Faulkner once said, "If you're going to write, write about human nature. That is the only thing that doesn't date." So don't worry about trends, and definitely don't write what you just saw in the theaters, because by the time you start, you're already two years behind. Write what you're dying to see at the theater.

Ron Bass: This is a big problem with my development team because I'd write a scene that I really like, then I'll get six faxes in the morning, and four of them will say they didn't like it. It tears at your confidence, but it forces you to look at the arguments in an objective way. Ultimately, if you really like what you wrote, you have final say. After listening to the comments and rereading the scene, maybe I'm wrong, but I have to listen to my own ear on this and trust my own judgment. You may be afraid, but it reinforces that feeling that you can't ever guide your star by other people's opinions. It also works the other way. If five people like it and one doesn't, but her argument makes sense to me, I'll go back and look at it, and find a different way of solving the problem. At the end of the day, you can only write to please yourself. Of course, you desperately want to please everybody, and hope everyone in the world will love it.

Steven de Souza: I'm not sure that "high concept" ideas are the best way to go. All those "How to Play the Hollywood Game" seminars that teach you how to sell a script in thirty days, or how to get past the reader, contribute largely to this 90 percent of crap. With a few exceptions, the most successful films are the ones that break the mold. The market goes in cycles. What happens when a movie is successful is, two years later you see a whole bunch of bad copies of that film, and when these imitations fail, the trend is declared dead.

Write what excites you, or what you think you can do a good job of delivering. It doesn't have to be a high concept. Look at *American Beauty*—an unpitchable sitcom about a dysfunctional family turned inside out, but amazingly well-executed, original, and fresh.

Akiva Goldsman: The trick is to write what you know, and be connected to the material of your imagination, thematically and concretely. In the case of my first script, what I knew was emotionally disturbed children and autism. I felt I could write about that well. The other trick is to write what interests you, because if you're not fascinated and excited by the writing of the script, the reader won't be fascinated and excited by the reading of it. I don't know why this is true. If the fun goes in, it comes out in the same way. If you write cynically, the reader will feel cynical. I always say that even episodes of *The Love Boat* were somebody's best work. Somebody sat there loving what they were doing, and that's what gave it the energy to move forward. In my case, I knew autism and I loved thrillers, so I combined them. People are too focused on that "high concept" idea. By writing what you know, I mean write what excites you and study it sufficiently so that your imagination can reside with some comfort in the unique world of your story. If it's well written, it will sell more than the stuff written by writers who think they know what'll sell.

Aline Brosh McKenna: Look at the kind of stories you yourself enjoy. What are the movies that you run out to see on the first day? Some people have a wide assortment of genres that they like, and some don't. Being in touch with yourself as an audience member is an important part of being a writer, learning to listen to your own inside voice telling you what you're interested in. That's the voice I try to listen to that leads me to the most interesting places.

One of the things about screenwriting is that there's a strong tradition of writing in genres. When I talk to people who are first starting out, I always advise them to pick a genre and innovate inside of the genre. Finding what's unique is finding your own voice.

Michael Schiffer: Too many beginners aim low. They think, "Hollywood never makes anything good, so I'll write some dumb comedy." That's not a good career strategy. I urge writers to aim as high as they can, to tell the most personal, or complex, or exciting story they can, so that the voice they bring is a worthy voice that'll make a difference. It's not a question of trying to be commercial, but writing the best possible version of your favorite kinds of movies. Without worrying about the market, write the kind of movies *you* want to see, and if they happen to be commercial, more power to you. It's fine to be a snobbish highbrow, but you've got to respect the fact that movies are a popular medium, and there's nothing wrong with writing movies that people like.

61. Have Something to Say

> *Art is a microscope which the artist fixes on the*
> *secrets of his soul and shows to people these secrets*
> *which are common to all.*
>
> —LEO TOLSTOY

The writing process is a search for meaning, a theme, what the story is *really* about, what gives it meaning and a purpose for being, besides making millions of dollars for stars and movie studios. Until you know what you're trying to say, your work isn't finished. All great writing is about something. With extrinsic motives aside, no professional screenwriter commits three months to a year on a script unless he has something to say. Because they're great observers and often sensitive souls, successful screenwriters are able to recognize and offer insights into the human condition.

As writer Dorothy Bryant puts it, "We are the voices for the deeper, unspoken dramas in other people's hearts." The key is being careful not to make it so obvious that it becomes preachy. As Darryl Zanuck once said, "If I want a message, I'll call Western Union!" Movie audiences are not looking to be lectured, they expect to be entertained. You can still educate and inspire, just do it in a subtle way.

Gerald DiPego: Sometimes you can have something you might call "pure entertainment," and theme is not very important. But if you want to do more than just entertain, if you want to entertain and enrich, inspire, or say something about the world and the human condition, then you have to think about what you want to say in order to subtly weave it through the story.

Derek Haas: Theme is always there. Sure, you have the idea for the movie, but what's this movie about? What are we saying to the audience? Is it about "a young man discovering who he is in the world?" Is it about "a boy learning responsibility rather than lawlessness?" Once you have the theme, every single scene relates to it in some way.

Michael Brandt: It's impossible to tell a compelling story without knowing what you're trying to say.

Amy Holden Jones: I write because I have something to say. Too many people want to be screenwriters but they have nothing to say, so all they can do is reference other movies.

Andrew W. Marlowe: If your story doesn't have a theme, you'll have to work harder to make it worth your audience's time, because as human beings, we look at stories to extract value from them. It's the reason why human beings have told stories since the dawn of time, starting around the fire, then going to plays, then print, then movies,

radio, and TV. We tell stories for a reason, which is our need to con-
textualize our experience. Theme is what lets us do that, because the
story is about something. If you have a story that's not about anything,
it's not going to be worth your audience's time and attention.

Bill Marsilii: I've never started writing a script without knowing
what it was really about, whether it's a character's redemption, or trying to regain their self-esteem, or trying to love again. Without theme,
I wouldn't know how to write it. Too many movies come out with
great special effects, but they're not about anything. They're soulless.

Aline Brosh McKenna: Good storytelling is all about theme. Always
think about it. Your story is the interaction between your character
and your theme. So if you don't know what your movie is about, you'll
have a terrible time figuring things out.

Terry Rossio: My experience is that one always starts with a theme
in mind, and as the story emerges, invariably a different theme asserts
itself as necessary and correct.

Eric Roth: Everything you write should reflect your theme. It's the first
thing I think of, and everything plays off of that. If your theme is "loneliness," for example, you try to show what makes these people lonely,
how it affects them, how they behave in the world because of it. Whether
it's intentional or unintentional, I think every story says something.

Michael Schiffer: Whenever possible, I'd like to think my audience
is smart, and I like to write not to the lowest denominator, but to
respect my audience and think, "Wouldn't it be great to go to movies and see smart people talking about smart stuff?" So I try to write
something that'll flatter the intellect of my audience and be as meaningful as I can make it, while simultaneously entertaining them and
sweeping them into the story.

62. Know What Makes a Great Story

Tell the readers a story! Because without a story,
you're merely using words to prove you can
string them together in logical sentences.
—ANNE MCCAFFREY

What makes a story great is entirely a subjective opinion. Some writers tell the novice that great stories are all about structure, with a clear beginning, middle, and end. Others teach you that it's interesting characters doing unexpected things against clear and compelling conflicts. Others maintain that you need a high-concept, commercial idea to make it in Hollywood. But at their core, all great stories must move an audience or a reader in some way.

Ron Bass: What makes a great story is the level of your response to it. Great stories make me feel in a way that's deep, original, and enjoyable, and they stay with me.

Leslie Dixon: To me, it's simply wanting to know what will happen next, all the way through. My husband was once a camp counselor where he learned how to tell stories by the campfire. You learn quickly how to keep the campers' attention, like throwing in a twist here and there, and making them wonder what will happen. All too often, writers never put themselves in the position of the audience going, "This is boring the crap out of me." They leave that to the reader who just tosses the script in the recycling bin.

Akiva Goldsman: What makes a great story is a resonance, and its ability, through the vibration that occurs between reader and object, to transport the reader from their life, and upon their return, give them some feeling that they know their life better, that there is some relationship to that which is common in human experience. This is why reading and watching movies, when they work, is wonderful. By going away, you come back richer by the alchemy of art. You're transformed into someone who has a firsthand understanding of things that were really alien to you, and you're given a newer understanding of your own experience.

Derek Haas: Surprise is a factor. You want to constantly throw surprises at the reader or the audience. Set up an expectation, and then squash it. Zig when they think you're going to zag.

Michael Brandt: Conflict, pace, and character growth. The head of a studio once boiled it down to this: What does your main character want at the beginning of the movie that he gets at the end of the movie?

Amy Holden Jones: A great story takes me to a particular environment and introduces me to characters who face seemingly insurmountable obstacles and find ways to surmount these obstacles in a surprising matter. Humor helps a lot. Basically, anything that entertains me.

Laeta Kalogridis: Characters I care about in a plot that puts them under pressure, revealing who they truly are in relation to themselves and each other.

Nicholas Kazan: You have no idea what happens next, you're continually surprised, you're satisfied by the surprises, and ultimately, the pleasures of the narrative resonate with deeper themes.

Scott Rosenberg: I have to be invested in the characters. To me, the greatest action movie ever made is *Die Hard,* not because of all the shit exploding, but because every time they cut back to Bonnie Bedelia's face, she knows it's her crazy husband who's doing everything he can to save her. It was this connection between the two characters that made me care. Another film where you care about the relationship is *48 Hrs.* With all the other ones, who cares? I despised movies like *Independence Day* and *Godzilla* and *Volcano.* I don't care what you do technically. If I don't care about the characters, I just don't care, period.

Terry Rossio: A great story first creates interest. Without that, the story has no power. A great story then translates that interest into either insight or emotion, or both.

Eric Roth: For me, the exciting thing about a story is that it takes you to some place you've never been before. And it's got to follow dramatic rules, even if it's more incidental than the traditional kind of story.

Michael Schiffer: Nobody really knows until it's all there. For me, a great story, whether a comedy or tragedy, is an authentic cauldron for which there's no psychological escape for the hero. Stories often leak on all sides. They're so poorly constructed that there are a million ways they don't hold up. But when something is locked down tight, there's no way out, and the stakes are real.

Tom Schulman: In the end, it's about some deep connection to something profound in us, touching us in some deep emotional way and resonating within us.

Ed Solomon: A great story is one that doesn't bore me, that makes me forget I'm sitting there listening to a story, or that makes me lose track of the fact that I'm in a movie theater, watching a movie.

CHAPTER 13

SCREENWRITING BASICS

63. Develop an Innate Sense of Drama and Conflict

All drama is conflict. Without conflict, you have no action. Without action, you have no character. Without character, you have no story. And without story, you ain't got no screenplay.

—SYD FIELD

Many scripts and pitches from beginning writers, with otherwise interesting elements, characters, or settings, simply fail on this issue alone, either because there's a complete lack of conflict, or not enough of it to warrant audience interest. You always hear that film is a visual medium. But more important, it's a dramatic medium. At its simplest, a story is about a hero we root for to achieve a goal despite obstacles standing in his way. Drama and conflict come from the obstacles. Without them, it wouldn't be a story.

Conflict is what heightens interest from an audience and charges the air with tension by transforming boring events into compelling moments. It's what audiences want in a story, even though in real life, we try to avoid conflict and live as peaceful and conflict-free a life as possible. Then again, stories are not real life. As Alfred Hitchcock said, "Drama is life with all the boring parts cut out of it."

Leslie Dixon: Conflict is simply having characters not get what they want.

Michael Schiffer: Good drama requires obstacles along the way, and if a section is very flat, one of the things a writer can ask is, "This is too easy for them; what could happen to make it absolutely difficult, painful, agonizing, impossible?" If you have a good story that goes from *A* to *B*, ask yourself what obstacles would make the journey from *A* to *B* more exciting and interesting to watch. The more legitimate and difficult the hindrance, and the more the characters care about reaching their goal, the more exciting the story.

Tom Schulman: Whenever I'm writing and my character gets happy, or everybody agrees with each other, I have a problem. I can only spend a couple of pages at that stage before I throw in some kind of conflict. You can spend a lot of time developing characters, but unless they come into conflict that will test them, there's nothing interesting happening.

Robin Swicord: You don't learn how to write a screenplay by just reading screenplays and watching movies. It's about developing the kind of mind that sees and makes drama. You can do this in a kind of holistic way by reading history and theology and psychology, reading great fiction, poetry, and plays. You develop an eye for the structures of everything and look for the patterns that help you become a dramatist.

64. Raise the Stakes

> *I would never write about someone who*
> *was not at the end of his rope.*
> —STANLEY ELKIN

Stakes, also known as the "dreadful alternative," are what the protagonists stand to win or lose if they achieve their main goal or fail. Will they die, will they lose their fortune, their freedom, the love of their life? This is crucial because if the characters aren't moved enough by the stakes to battle obstacles, if dire consequences aren't established, how can you expect an audience to care? In fact, most scripts are rejected because the stakes aren't compelling enough. When stakes are high, and both sides are unyielding, you have intense drama.

Gerald DiPego: Whenever someone asks me to read a script, or I'm developing my own, I always ask myself, "What's at stake here?" If you lose sight of that, you'll eventually lose your audience. And not only do you need to know what's at stake, but it has to rise, things have to get worse during the course of your story. If you're in the middle of the story and everyone is having a great time with no conflict anywhere, how can you expect an audience to be involved?

Michael Schiffer: There are very few movies where nothing happens. You want the stakes, as the hero perceives them, to be as high as possible. The kind of movie usually defines the kind of stakes. For instance, in an action adventure, the stakes are physical jeopardy, or in a movie like *American Beauty*, the stakes are psychological, the survival of the spirit. Even in a comedy, the stakes are high and serious to the characters but funny to the audience. You want your characters to be at risk and have things of great importance to them to be at stake.

65. Realize the Importance of Characters

> *The whole thing is, you've got to make them care about somebody.*
>
> —Frank Capra

Storytelling is all about characters. People don't go to the movies to see scary, romantic, or exciting situations; they go to see memorable human beings reacting to scary, romantic, or exciting situations. Which means your goal as a screenwriter is to create characters that the audience will identify with. It goes beyond simply revealing their traits and emotions on the page and making your protagonist "likable." This is about *caring*, even if the character is immoral: caring about the character's personality, attitude, goals, flaws, and rooting for him or her to succeed against all odds.

Ron Bass: To me, there's no distinction between story and character because most stories are about what happens between people. If the story is about someone climbing a mountain or facing some physical hazard alone, then that's different, but in most of the stories that I see, that I write, that I care about, story is what happens as characters interact, so character is story.

Gerald DiPego: Let's say you have an idea that starts out like, "I just thought of a great new way to rob a bank. I'm going to build a movie around that." If you don't throw your focus on who these people are, what their dreams and demons are, you'll be on the road to a neat idea that ends up empty, because that's who's sitting in the audience—people. If you can connect them to your characters in a meaningful way, then the audience will have a complete experience with your film, and they'll still appreciate all the stunts, clever twists, and dialogue while operating on a deeper level because they care about your characters.

Jim Kouf: Your characters have to be so interesting and compelling you can't wait to get an actor attached. After all, why do people sit through certain movies? Because the dialogue is great, and something about the characters makes you love them or hate them. It's just like life. Why do you sit with a few people and have a conversation, and other people, you decline when they invite you to dinner?

Andrew W. Marlowe: What makes us flawed is what makes us human, and it's what makes characters attractive to the audience. The fact that Rick Blaine in *Casablanca* is disengaged and so emotionally wounded that he doesn't want to care is what makes that movie worth watching. Here's a guy who has to be dragged kicking and screaming to invest in anything, who doesn't want to stick his neck out for anybody until the love of his life walks through the door.

Characters are like icebergs: 90 percent of the work you'll do on a character will never be seen, but it supports the 10 percent that we'll see on the page. I'm not talking about character biographies, but of knowing who your character really is and why he has to take this journey through the story, what his hopes and dreams and fears are, what his emotional investments are, who broke his heart, how he deals with life, and so on . . . that's what your first ten minutes should be about in a story—getting to know your main character.

Tom Schulman: Aristotle was right. Plot determines who your characters are. But once you've figured out who your characters are, they become more important than the plot. Without characters, nobody cares about the story. I always try to drive my characters toward a story.

66. Read Your Dialogue Out Loud

If you read your work out loud, it helps to know what's bad.
—GARRISON KEILLOR

Writing authentic, well-crafted dialogue that sparkles, individualizes characters, and entertains the reader is the ultimate challenge for screenwriters, who otherwise may have solid script elements. It's crucial to attracting talent, which can green-light your script. Writing great dialogue can also sell the writer, for those who excel in this area are highly sought after to the tune of six figures per week for dialogue rewrites.

That said, dialogue is not as important as character development or structure because you're not writing a play. Screenwriting is mostly about what you see, not hear. Remember that you're writing motion pictures, not visual radio, and all the witty dialogue in the world won't sell your script if it fails on everything else.

Bottom line, you want as little dialogue as possible, but whatever dialogue is on the page, it must be great. Reading your dialogue out loud is a useful habit to test it. You'll be amazed at the difference between reading it and hearing it. You'll not only hear what your lines sound like to other people but also see if the character's uniqueness comes through in that person's speech.

Akiva Goldsman: Sometimes, I do read my dialogue out loud, especially when I'm brain-fried, though I'm glad no one's around to see this. Ultimately, I've been really lucky to be on sets, so I often get to hear my dialogue spoken by professional actors. This never stops being a thrill.

Derek Haas: You should be able to look at some page in the middle of the script and know which character is speaking just by reading a dialogue block. Each character should have his or her own voice.

Keep an ear out for the way people speak when you're in a coffee shop, having dinner, or out in the street.

Michael Brandt: The best dialogue sounds natural. You should be able to read it aloud and then transcribe that cadence to your characters. We use contractions when we speak, we stop in mid-sentence, we change what we were going to say halfway through speaking. Not everyone can speak like a poet or a professor.

Ed Solomon: Most people feel a great joy when they write something quickly, because they're unable to distinguish between the elation of transcribing their thoughts onto the page and the joy that comes from actually organizing thoughts in a way that will have some meaning for someone else. Sometimes, we feel something is great because it felt great to write it. So it's valuable to have a reading of your script, and listen to it with other people in the room. Further, if you're really serious about it, stage a few scenes from it, and direct them. Put yourself through what would seem like a ridiculous exercise. It's a good way to get a feeling for how a scene really works. Those of us who've had movies made have had the benefit of seeing how some things work and others don't. Sometimes it's really painful to hear your words read.

Robin Swicord: I read my dialogue out loud all the time. That's how you know if someone would really say something. If you can't say it, cut it.

CHAPTER 14

THE MOST IMPORTANT AUDIENCE

67. Realize the Reader Is Your First Audience

It isn't what happens to people on a page—it's what happens to a reader in his heart and mind.

—GORDON LISH

Professional writers never forget that they're writing for a reader, that their ultimate duty is to seduce them by creating that *wow!* feeling on as many pages as possible and to interest them so intensely that they forget they're reading words on a page. That's what great writing is all about.

But most aspiring screenwriters seem to forget that someone will actually read their script, the gatekeeper that stands between them and the executive who can make things happen, whether it's an agent, producer, actor, or director. The gatekeepers wield remarkable influence. If they say this is the most amazing script they've ever read, their bosses will read it on their lunch hour. But if they dislike something, that's it; it's over. And yet, they're still on your side, for every time they pick up a script, they hope it's the winning one, the one that'll eventually become a box-office champ and make them look good for discovering it. But to do so, your script must *wow!* them first.

Ron Bass: You definitely write a script knowing someone's going to read it. I'm probably more conscious than most writers of the prose descriptions between dialogue. It's something I spend a lot of time and care on because I feel that's when I communicate *intent* to the reader, who may be the studio executive, the director, or the actress. When it's not clear, I want them to know what my characters are thinking and feeling between the lines, because you can't see the actor performing. You're only reading the words. And without eliminating all ambiguity and irony in the scene, what you say between the lines helps the reader get the idea and the feeling of the atmosphere of what's going on, compensating for the fact that you're not watching the movie.

Michael Brandt: Write for the reader. The first twenty times your script is read, it won't be by a director, an actor, or the head of a studio. It'll be by a reader who has a stack of hundreds of scripts to read. You have to show him or her the movie on the page, and that means forgetting all the bullshit rules and just writing to entertain the hell out of the reader. Make it come to life on the page.

Steven de Souza: The best piece of advice I got is, "You've got to get them in the first ten pages." You must keep in mind that you're always writing for the reader first, not a movie audience that'll see the collaboration of two hundred people a year later. Also, you learn over time to be less camera-happy in describing all the camera angles. I wince reading my early stuff—I'm actually recommending lenses!

Tom Schulman: I simply focus on making the story as interesting and exciting as possible, which includes the reader, who I imagine is actually watching the movie and I'm just describing on the page what they see. So I don't differentiate between reader and viewer.

Ed Solomon: Be careful, because the more you write a script like a final film, the more difficult it is for readers and studio executives to conceive of it as a film. What you get from a film when you watch it is a different experience than when you read it. Edited film has a certain meaning when you watch it. The closer you get to writing a final film, the more difficult it'll be to get it by the decision-makers, because their gut feeling when they read the script is often different from the literal filmic translation. It's not always as satisfying when it's made into a movie. The same works the other way. If you took a great movie and transcribed it from the screen to a script and then tried to sell it to a studio executive, it wouldn't be as satisfying a visceral experience.

68. Avoid Sin Number One: Being Dull

No one ever sold anybody anything by boring them to death.
—DAVID OGILVY

Whereas the previous habit of thinking of your reader is more about presenting a professional script and a positive reading experience, this habit covers a wider arena, encompassing not only the entertainment and emotional experience of an audience but also an attitude in general.

Most beginners fail to realize that what's interesting to them may be dull for a mass audience. Every time you sit down to write, you should be afraid of losing the reader at any moment. The worst sin in Hollywood is for the reader of a script to say, "So what?" No reader recommends a boring script, no executive green-lights a boring movie (unless, of course, a major star wants to make it) and no audience pays eleven dollars to be bored for two hours. To paraphrase playwright William Gibson, "The first business of the screenwriter is to keep the audience from walking out."

Derek Haas: Put the same amount of creativity into your action descriptions as you do into your dialogue. I can't tell you how many times I've read a beginner's script where the dialogue had some spark to it and then you get to the action-descriptions and find these staccato, clipped, declarative sentences: "He turns on the light. He crosses the room. He sits down." Christ, bring some life to it! Bring a voice to it.

Another common mistake is basing the script on a bad idea. The writing might be adequate, but the *idea* behind the script is boring, trite, derivative, or silly. Brian Koppelman said it best when he offered advice to young writers: "Calculate less." Quit trying to write the "next" whatever—the next *Hangover*! The next *Inception*! Just write the story you want to write. Make it your own thing and make it great.

Michael Brandt: The biggest problem with beginning scripts is pace. Every scene starts too early and ends too late. It's the "coffee cup conversation factor." Beginners will write about two people entering the room, making some coffee, putting the sugar in it, then the cream. Then they both take a sip, mmm, it's good, then they put the cup down and have a conversation. A good writer will just start with them putting the coffee cups down. Or a car chase works too.

Jim Kouf: No one wants to sit through a dull movie, and no one in Hollywood wants to read a dull script. I write to entertain. I want to keep people turning the page, whatever it takes, so that they don't put the script down. I just want to tell a good story in the best possible way, and have someone become committed to the material based on the writing. The characters have to come alive. It's not real life we're putting down. This is heightened reality—people are a lot wittier, funnier, and larger than they are in real life.

Andrew W. Marlowe: Good storytelling is not a flat line. Even Shakespeare knew that after a tense scene he'd have to bring the jokers in and let the audience off the hook for a second. I find contrast to be extraordinarily important in a story. For instance, if someone is about to get bad news, it's a lot more impactful if the person is coming out of a party. There's a great moment in *Toto le Héros* [Toto the Hero], a birthday party at the guy's office, and everyone's laughing, and he takes a phone call where he learns that somebody has died. And while you see his face drop, you hear all these people laugh all around him, which makes the moment all that much more devastating.

Now you don't need to have a contrast that vast in every scene, but having contrast helps in keeping things fresh for your audience. They think the story is going one way but it goes a different way, or you try to follow scenes of intensity with scenes of quiet, so that the heartbeat of the story changes, because if the heartbeat is the same, it becomes a sort of metronome for the audience, and they'll eventually check out. You have to give them time to breathe, time to engage. There's a life to scripts you need to take advantage of, and that life comes from contrast.

Michael Schiffer: It's really cool if your characters are among the most vivid people you've ever known. We're not that vivid and colorful every minute of our lives. So what I try to do in successive drafts, once the story is sketched in, is wonder with each line of dialogue, "Is this the most interesting, vivid, and colorful way to say this? How can I boost this up so that the people I'm watching are people I wish I encountered every day in my life?"

To do that you have to constantly question every line and every character and intensify every single, boring moment in your script. Ask yourself, "Would I want to be at a dinner party with this person? Good guys or bad guys, are they interesting enough to be in my life?" If they're not, make them more interesting. You owe your audience the gift of good company.

69. Evoke an Emotional Response

> *I want readers of my scripts to feel my scenes.*
> —SHANE BLACK

Despite the wealth of information devoted to the principles of screenwriting, from books, magazines, and blogs, to seminars and websites, to film schools, story consultants, and screenwriting gurus, a surprising lack of awareness still exists among aspiring writers about what great screenwriting is really about—creating a satisfying emotional experience in the reader.

Hollywood is in the emotion-delivery business. It trades in human emotions, delivering emotional experiences carefully packaged in movies and television to the tune of $10 billion per year. If you doubt this, take a look at how it advertises its films in newspapers. When was the last time you saw a movie ad that said, "*Well structured, great plot points, fresh dialogue?*" No, what you always see are promises of the emotions you'll feel by watching the movie. Make sure your script matches these promises to a reader.

Gerald DiPego: Most movies fail because they don't reach inside the audience. They feel empty because they're written from the outside, and they don't ask you to invest anything or care about the characters, so it's not a complete experience.

Terry Rossio: There are many people who are creative but can't write, and a truckload of projects out there which are highly original and thoroughly unappealing. What Hollywood needs from a screenwriter is someone who can invent stories that are moving, compelling, and engender interest.

Eric Roth: The drama of the story certainly dictates what's emotional, and you try to make your characters act in such a human way that's recognizable by an audience, and therefore universally understood. Even in the most outlandish situations, sometimes it's the little human touches that bring everyone together. If it makes me feel something when I write it, I'm hoping that I'm translating that to the audience. For me, it's about setup and payoff. I try to set things up so that they pay off in a way I hope evokes a strong emotional reaction.

Michael Schiffer: Whether it's comedy or drama, our entire goal as writers is to make our audience respond to the emotions of the characters by pulling them through terrible situations that reflect their own conflicts. When an audience connects, they have a cathartic reaction. Their emotions are purged, because they all have stress and pain in their lives. When they can identify with actors who go through these things and triumph, they feel renewed and full of hope. It then becomes a communal experience that makes an audience know we all share a common bond.

Tom Schulman: All you try to do is involve an audience in the drama of other people's lives—their relationships, their obsessions, who they are, where they are—and if they're identifiable and they start out in conflict, theoretically, the audience should be hooked on that roller coaster. So emotion should be the result of what you've set up, not the other way around.

● ● ●

If you've studied and mastered all the habits up to now and have written a great script, don't even bother with the next chapter on marketing. Why? Because if you truly have a great screenplay, you could literally drop it in a Beverly Hills park and it will get made. But since the odds are that your script is not perfect, let's find out how you can market your skills while writing your next script. You'd better be writing your next script! If not, go back to Chapter 2 and start over. You shouldn't even bother with marketing until you have at least three quality scripts.

PART 5

MARKETING

It's Not Who You Know, It's Your Writing

*The most important part in filmmaking is
played by the writers. We must do everything
in our power to keep them from finding out.*

—Irving Thalberg

CHAPTER 15

THE HOLLYWOOD SYSTEM

70. Understand the Hollywood System

There are fewer stars for writers on the Hollywood
Walk of Fame than there are for animals.

—Aljean Harmetz

Aspiring writers are generally sheltered from the realities of the industry; all they know from entertainment news sources are the glamorous articles and the sound bites about projects sold, dollar amounts, and players involved. It's only after selling something and being thrown into the system that they discover the realities they must adapt to.

Although a good screenplay is the hottest commodity in the industry, people in this business who don't know you aren't going to be impressed by the fact that you actually wrote one. It's an interesting paradox that writers are essential to the survival of the industry and yet are undervalued. This is an industry where your work is trashed, where you get rewritten, where you're fired without knowing it, where a stable of lawyers works diligently to make sure your payments are delayed, and so on. Until you sell a script, or at the very least win a major contest or are represented by a legitimate agency, you don't exist. If executives think your product will advance their career, they'll like you. If they don't, they'll ignore you.

Remember the shock Robin Swicord experienced when she saw just how many scripts there were on just one executive's office shelves? Now multiply this by the number of offices in town and you'll only get the number of *current* scripts awaiting a decision. Based on

Writers Guild statistics, you could safely estimate that, not including assignments, about 50,000 spec screenplays are written and registered every year.

As some of you may already know, and at the risk of alienating sensitive artists, Hollywood only exists to make money. The industry is basically a collection of profit-minded mega-corporations whose main product is the motion picture and who invest a lot of money to produce, distribute, and ultimately screen it through various venues. This is a business, not an art gallery; no one spends $100 million on a piece of art without expecting to recoup all costs and make a profit in order to make more films.

To justify their salaries, most development executives, in addition to finding great material and attaching writers to it, believe they must change a script, even when it doesn't need any changing. They can't subscribe to the "If it ain't broke, don't fix it" theory. For development executives, it has to be "If it ain't broke, break it," and that's why the process you enter as soon as you sell a script is called "development hell."

As writer John Gregory Dunne once said, "Writers are used and discarded like so many wads of Kleenex," until a star or a director becomes attached, and then it's a go-picture. That's the Hollywood system, for better and worse, and you have to sink or swim in these shark-infested waters. You have to know how to play by the rules before you can break them.

Steven de Souza: It's always the unexpected stuff that works, the one that breaks the rules, that's contrary to what "they" say. The biggest mistake studio executives make is not going to the movies enough in a movie theater *with an audience.* If you want to know what audiences want, what they like, go to the movies with an audience. You may see a lousy movie, but there's always one place in it where all of a sudden, the audience is on the edge of their seat. This may be a little hint of what your movie should be. Because things change. The audience is getting smarter and smarter and savvier to movies in general, and so we have to be as sophisticated. If you can't surprise yourself, you won't surprise an audience.

Laeta Kalogridis: Almost any movie you see has gone through a meat-grinder development process. Just because many movies seem poorly written, people new to this work assume the writers them-selves must be terrible (and consequently, that getting work will be easy.) Neither of these things is necessarily true.

Nicholas Kazan: What you must understand about studio execu-tives is that their prime job isn't to get your script made, but to keep their jobs. If you have a script that's kind of good, they can't take the chance. The last thing they want to do, if you're an unknown writer, is walk into their boss's office and say, "This script is really good," and have their boss read it, and say, "This script is terrible, what were you thinking?" That happens three times and they're out of a job. So they only want to walk in with nothing less than a brilliant script that'll make them look good. A good script isn't good enough. You need a really great script with a subject that's idiosyncratic. But if you write a great script, and it's a cop buddy movie, quality may not be enough because there are so many similar scripts.

Another important thing to know is that executives are incredibly overworked. Between story meetings and scripts they have to read, they need to make hundreds of phone calls a day. They don't have time to focus. It's a miracle they can work this hard and this long with any degree of efficiency. You can't expect to stay in their minds, espe-cially if you're an unknown.

Scott Rosenberg: In the studio system, everyone's job is to say no. Everyone is a gatekeeper, guarding the palace from the mobs out there. But the fact is that all anyone really wants to do is say yes. Everyone's looking for that amazing project, and when there's an amazing script, everybody in town hears about it. Everyone pricks up their ears when there's a hot new writer in town. The reality is, all you need to do is write a good script. I know it sounds so glib, but it's a reality. I know because most of my friends are the ones dying for great material.

When I first came out here [to Los Angeles], I wasn't trying to push my script. I was just too busy to write because I was embarrassed. Everyone I met was a would-be screenwriter. I remember one time, I was invited to dinner at this executive's house, and he asked me what I wanted to do, and I said I wanted to be a screenwriter. He said, "My landscaper wants to be a screenwriter. And you see that guy over there? That's José, my gardener. He wants to be a screenwriter. And see that guy who's doing my pool? He wants to be a screenwriter, and over there, that's my wife, Suzy. She wants to be a screenwriter." I was so embarrassed that from then on, when asked, I'd tell people I hunt Nazis. Anything not to be a screenwriter.

Terry Rossio: In Hollywood, story content of movies follows a hierarchy of power, not the relative quality of various ideas. Hollywood does not lack for quality writing. It's just that quality writing commonly has to be sacrificed in order to propel a film into production. A studio needs a star and a director to make a film, so those are the folk who'll define content. If they don't have the same creative sensibilities, then the content will change.

Ed Solomon: It's a hard world because there's a lot of duplicity. People say one thing and mean another. They use flattery as a kind of lubricant and it works because we are highly sensitive to it. We tend to blend people's opinions of our work with opinions of us. But most of the time they don't mean it, so we find ourselves confused. We don't really know what's true anymore.

Robin Swicord: My great disappointment was not understanding how unimportant the studio system of "perfecting" a screenplay really was. A lot of the so-called development is really about buying time for the studio. It's more about trying this or trying that. They don't always view the writers as the dramatic experts in the room, and that's a mistake because you end up having really good writers taking notes from people who don't know what they're talking about.

So it was really a surprise to me that they would assemble these writers, who've been doing nothing for a decade except writing, and not listen to what they had to say, and then excuse them from the room when it came time to do the real work of casting, shooting the movie, editing, and so forth. It would be like asking I. M. Pei to design a building and when the blueprints are first laid out on the table, fire him and bring in various subcontractors to make decisions about the building. It's amazing to me that this process still goes on the way it does. It's not a system that works to make good movies.

71. Learn the Business

In Hollywood, information is power.
To make it in the entertainment industry,
you'll have to know what's happening—to whom,
where, when, how, and why. On a global basis.
—LINDA BUZZELL, *HOW TO MAKE IT IN HOLLYWOOD*

Quick! Can you name the heads of every studio in town? How about the directors of development at the major production companies? If not, you've got some studying to do. You need to know who the players are—the agents, directors, executives, producers, screenwriters (you now know twenty-two of them), where they are and what they like, and what movies they're associated with. This is the time to put on your businessperson's cap and learn the market.

Read as much as you can. Read the trades and online blogs—but not every day, or you'll become jaded and frustrated with the feeling that everyone is working except you. Surf the web. Most studios, film production companies, and celebrities have informative websites or strong social media presence. You can learn by watching shows like *Entertainment Tonight* and *Access Hollywood*. Some recent films about the film industry include *The Player, Get Shorty, Swimming with Sharks, The Big Picture, Bowfinger,* and *The Muse*. A few classics include *Sunset Boulevard* and *The Bad and the Beautiful*. And of course, since the best way to learn something is to be immersed in it, getting a job in the industry would be valuable.

Eric Roth: It's very helpful to know, as best you can, who holds the power and who doesn't. It's always better to work with someone who can say yes than one who can't. Try to work with those who are highest at the studio, or with people who have some say over it when it's done. You'd rather work for someone who's more successful than not. But there are no rules. Don't misunderstand me; I'm not that Machiavellian. But there's a certain kind of material that appeals to a certain kind of executive, so you have to know these things. And you get to know this by being in this town a lot, or reading the trades, or paying attention to who's doing what. You sort of get a smell for what the market will do or not do.

Robin Swicord: You have to understand how the business works. Sometimes, I'm so mystified I can't believe this is a business. You have to understand that the tide comes in and the tide goes out. There's a constant shift of personalities. Some studios are more stable than others, and you have to note which ones are which. You learn this by picking up what my husband calls the "sports pages of the industry," either *Variety*, *The Hollywood Reporter,* or Nikki Finke's *Deadline Hollywood*.

The problem with reading the trades is that a lot of information is planted by publicists, so it seems everyone but you is making a big deal somewhere, or they're associated with some wonderful project that's just been announced. You can't help but get into a state of envy. It's good to pick up the trades every now and then but not every day.

Another way to learn is by talking to your agent or lawyer, or by going through horrendous experiences on projects, like one studio telling me, "We want to write a musical. We believe that musicals could be back in and Cher wants to be in a musical and if you can write the screenplay in six weeks and give blood every single day at our blood bank, you can be the lucky writer who writes a musical for Cher." What I wanted to know was, "Does Cher know she wants to do a musical? Has anyone talked to Cher? Let me talk to Cher's agents before I get excited."

Check out the sources on everything that's brought to you because you know you're the only one who'll do the hard work for the longest time. So they'd better be ready to back it up, have the rights squared away if it's a book, let me have a reasonable period of time to write the script, or have a good enough reputation that agents won't run away from them. Always make sure you put yourself into the best possible environment.

CHAPTER 16

NETWORKING

72. Live in Los Angeles

*Life is like a fishing trip—if you want to catch a big fish,
you've got to go where the big fish are.*
—OLD HOLLYWOOD SAYING, QUOTED BY PETER MILLER

Writers often ask whether you could have a screenwriting career outside Los Angeles. The answer is clear: You can write screenplays and hone your craft from anywhere in the world. In fact, it's preferable to live outside Los Angeles while you write. You'll feel more creative. And in this digital age, thanks to e-mail and PDF files, you could even market your scripts from out of town.

But once you get interest from agents and producers, once your hot script sells, you should be in town because of all the meetings your agent will send you to for "meet-and-greets," pitches, and open assignments. Once you break in, your screenwriting life will revolve around producers and studio execs, not the other way around.

Ron Bass: As a beginner, and even as an established professional, I think it's very useful to be here, because of the meetings you have to take and generally interacting with the people you'll be collaborating with. There's just so much that can be done over the phone, and I think it's harder if you're not in L.A.

Michael Brandt: I hate to say it, but you should live in Los Angeles if you want to break into this business. Of course there are exceptions, but you're making it that much more difficult on yourself by not living here. You meet and hang out with so many people who are in the business when you live here. Everywhere you turn is someone who works at CAA [Creative Arts Agency] or WME [William Morris Endeavor] or Universal. All these people can help you if you've written a great script.

Laeta Kalogridis: If you're in TV, you have to live here. Otherwise, it depends on the person. It's easier for working, definitely, and for understanding the business.

Jim Kouf: You've got to know somebody who knows somebody, and you've got to be here. If you want to be in movies, in the business, you've got to be in L.A. I mean I'm not here because I love it here. I escape to Montana as often as I can. But there's a certain amount of time that I have to be here. I've got to meet with people, see them face-to-face; you always have to work at being employed. That's a tougher job than writing.

Michael Schiffer: There are many advantages to living here, although you don't have to. You can learn an awful lot about moviemaking, and therefore screenwriting. You can take acting classes, meet other young writers, and share each other's scripts. I don't know where else, except New York, you'll find a higher concentration of creative people making this their life's work. And in the business, it helps to take meeting after meeting, because you have to knock on a lot of doors before you can find someone who wants to hire you, and it's harder to imagine working with someone from Minnesota.

Tom Schulman: You certainly don't want to live here if you're writing. But as far as marketing, there are only two places where scripts are bought, and that's primarily Los Angeles, and to a lesser degree, New York. So unless you know someone in Los Angeles, it's just common sense to be here so that you can make the kinds of contacts that'll help sell your scripts.

73. Know the Importance of Relationships

> *Knowledgeable people know facts. Successful and*
> *prosperous people know people.*
>
> —John Demartini

Success for many screenwriters has come through a network of supporters, mentors, friends, advocates, and champions of their work. It's well known that Hollywood is an industry that runs on relationships. As a result, many aspiring writers believe they must focus on making them. What they don't realize is that when it comes to screenwriters, it's their writing samples that get them assignments, not the fact that they happened to be seen at a Hollywood party (see next habit). Although networking isn't as crucial for writers as the quality of their scripts, it's still an important habit to cultivate in order to create a network of supporters that'll welcome and champion your work when it crosses their desk. Networking should be seen as sowing the seeds for win-win relationships. It's all about helping other people achieve their goals, who in turn will help you achieve yours. You win when they provide access to your material. They win when you supply them with the great material they so desperately need.

Gerald DiPego: It's very important to create relationships within the industry, but I'm not very good at it. I was very shy when I started, but I tried to push through that. I came out here wanting to write industrial films as a day job, while I tried to sell a script or get hired to write features, so every time I called an industrial film producer to see what was out there, I'd also ask if they knew someone on the feature side, and I did this until somebody said they knew someone who was looking for scripts.

Leslie Dixon: Many relationships came to me because my first produced script was a hit. When this happens everyone wants to take you out to dinner or take meetings, so I met a lot of people from the get-go. But I've never been a schmoozing relationship chaser. There are people who shamelessly do this, and some of them succeed. It's a very male trait. Women don't tend to act like Sammy Glick–type people.

But I have to say the writers that do it will have more success than the ones who sit at home like a hermit. I recommend it. It's a quality I wish I had more of, but I'm just too proud to start up faux friendships, saying to myself, "I bet my career would be better if I was best friends with Steven Spielberg."

Your hustle should depend on how much money you banked away. If you have a family to support and the well runs dry, you have to be responsible for your career. You can't count on your agent to do everything. You have to combine quality work with exhausting networking. There are writers who write script after script, then go to all the parties they can, they're out pitching every five minutes. On the other hand, there's a point where this much activity can cheapen your stock.

Akiva Goldsman: I was very unconnected in Hollywood, but I had a friend from college who was an assistant at ICM, so I sent my script to him, and he read it and gave me notes. This process went on for months, and at one point, it was just laying on his desk and this agent picked it up and read it. Next thing I know, I get a call that they'd like to represent me.

Laeta Kalogridis: The friend who showed my script to an agent was a fellow student. I didn't even know he knew agents. He'd been an assistant before he came to UCLA and worked briefly at CAA before deciding against an agent career. If you're going to network, I find it more useful to hang out with people who are your peers, because you'll all rise together.

Nicholas Kazan: It's very important to have friends and to know development people because they'll be more favorably inclined toward your script. All you need is someone who'll look forward to your script, which may be the fifteenth in a pile of thirty. The only way to gain an edge, no matter how small, is to go on top of the pile, or be taken out and put aside to read first thing in the morning because the reader knows you. And you get this edge because you met someone at a party, or it's a friend of a friend or whatever. It's a small edge over the competition.

I came to Los Angeles in 1976 with a group of friends and just hung out with the same people, who gradually became more successful, and through these people, I met more people. I was single and made all kinds of friends in the first five years I was here. But I didn't do it consciously or in a calculated move in order to network. Anything you do in a calculated way hurts you. If you don't make friends easily, I wouldn't try to network, because you won't make *real* friends. They'll see right through you. You can't pretend to like people you don't like in order to help your career.

Andrew W. Marlowe: Realize that when you first start out, the first round of pitches is not about selling your script. It's all about establishing relationships with these development executives. Think of it as a first step in your career, which is about connecting with executives who'll one day become the heads of studios. So focus on being enthusiastic and forget about selling because they're not in a position to buy it right now. What they do have is the power to recommend you and your writing to their bosses, and keep you in mind for future assignments when they need someone who doesn't cost them a lot of money. If you knock it out of the ballpark, the sale is gravy, but that's not why you're walking into the room. If you think of the sale, you're putting too much pressure on yourself. So walk into the room knowing that you made it into the first level, and that's a good thing.

Bill Marsilii: You can't just ask someone who's never met you to read your script. When you walk up to a total stranger with a 110-page screenplay in your hand, shove at it them and say, "Would you please read my script?" it's like asking a stranger, "Hi, you don't know me, but would you help me move this weekend?" You're really asking for five hours of somebody's time—time to read it, to prepare notes, and the time they'll spend with you over the phone trying to talk you off the ledge. When it comes to connecting with others who are in a position to help you, you should look at it this way: It's an imposition to be asked for a favor, but it's flattering to be asked for advice.

There's this great indie movie, *The Tao of Steve*, in which the main character happens to be an overweight slacker who somehow has an incredible success rate with women. He offers the following three rules of seduction, which I find appropriate for marketing your screenplay: 1. Eliminate desire (because if you're desperate, they can smell it on you.) 2. Be excellent in their presence (be interested in them, ask intelligent questions, know their work). Then after you've done both of these things, 3. Withdraw (leave them intrigued, wanting to know more about you or your story, until they're asking *you* if they could read your script).

Aline Brosh McKenna: Young writers seem to forget that people in the industry are desperate for good material. The business isn't constructed to keep you out of it, but to bring you into it. More than ever now, there are so many contests and agents and producers. It's a world that's so desperate for good writers. So if you can build it, they'll be there. If you write something great, and you know somebody who is even peripherally involved in the industry, like the assistant director's brother-in-law's niece, it'll find its way to someone. It may not get green-lit and turned into a blockbuster immediately, but it'll get read, and if it's really good, it'll start your career. In my case, I had a college friend who was a year ahead of me who became a junior agent, so when my script was ready to show, I asked him if he knew any agents who might want to represent me.

Eric Roth: I think a lot of the work you get is from relationships. I've always had the sense that relationships were a key part of a career because my parents were in the business, and because of the nature of who I am. I recognize that people would rather work with someone they enjoy being with than not. But even though I wasn't consciously trying to make them, I wasn't afraid of relationships, so they kind of happened. Being savvy in who to work with or not, and being a gambler, I have a sort of street sense and try to put myself in the best position, where I feel the work has the best chance of getting done.

Writers only get a certain percentage of their screenplays produced, so you try to limit whatever makes it hardest to get things done. It's a sort of educated and calculated choice. If I have three attractive projects to choose from, and they're all equal, then I'll go with the one that has the best chance of getting made.

74. Understand That Your Writing, Not Your Charm, Gets You Work

It all starts on the page.
—Steven Spielberg

Up to now, we've seen many obvious habits that are often ignored by beginners. There is, however, one habit that beginning writers mistakenly overdevelop, often at the expense of quality material—the belief that networking will make them successful writers. You've just heard from established screenwriters that it's important. But the key word is "established." In other words, established writers have a reputation preceding them.

If you're a beginner, no amount of networking will sell your script or get you an assignment, at least in legitimate circles. It may get you read, which is useful if your material is up to par. If it isn't, you're burning the bridge with the potential buyer you've spent time schmoozing. You only have one chance to shine. The screenwriter is lucky to be the only element in the industry that doesn't need to network, because his writing has to speak for itself. Focus on raising the quality of your material instead of raising the number of your contacts.

Steven de Souza: When I was a story editor, I shared a suite at Universal with a writer who was obsessed with "networking." His first draft would always be his last draft. He never had time to do the polishing because he just had to have lunch with this person who just got promoted to that studio position, and so on. My bulletin board would be a set of three-by-five cards with the latest story I was blocking out. His bulletin board was full of articles from the trades about all the people he knew who got promoted.

There was an inverse proportion of the amount of time he spent working the town to the amount of work he got, whereas I just kept my nose to the grindstone. To this day, I still meet people who've been around as long as I have and I've never met them because I don't go out much; I write. Networking is important in order to find out about opportunities, but at the end of the day, it won't make you a better writer or enable you to sell a weak script. Networking is not a guarantee for a career. It's a guarantee to get a lot of Christmas cards and some invitations to premieres. It's better to know someone who's directing a play in some little theater and who's looking for material for a workshop. Even if you're writing a movie, you get out there and tell them you've got what they're looking for.

Scott Rosenberg: Here's the thing about me: I'm absolutely the most social screenwriter alive. I don't say this to brag. I'm actually a little ashamed of it. I go to these Hollywood parties when I'm here and I look around, and there's not one screenwriter there except me. Do you know why most of my friends are the heads of studios, agents, managers, and executives? Because all the other writers are home writing. The reality is that no one has ever said, "I'm gonna do a Scott Rosenberg movie because I hung out with him at a party last night." It's all about the writing. My charm is never going to get me a job. Some of the most brilliant writers out here are the most low-functioning socially. You can't stand to be in a room with them, but their work is just brilliant.

Ed Solomon: Relationships are crucial. However, how people go about having solid relationships is often misunderstood. People think that by networking they make better relationships. This is not the case. By networking, you get your name out more, but you also establish yourself on a subconscious level as someone who needs to network. You have to be careful about maintaining a kind of cachet for yourself that involves people perceiving you as someone who has something to offer them.

Often, people who have a lot to offer are not always out trying to sell themselves. If networking to you is about gaining information and understanding what's out there, I guess it could be valuable. But if networking is about getting yourself out there to sell yourself, you'll come across as just that. In a way, you're already networking simply by existing in this business. Your scripts are always out there networking on your behalf. As a new writer, my agents always told me to get out and meet a lot of people. However, in legitimate circles, no one will meet you unless they've already read your material. Your writing always precedes you. It all comes down to writing a great script, or showing real talent through a not-so-great but original script. People who go to parties only prove that they're good at going to parties.

People only want to work with people who can help elevate their own career. Everyone knows that people you meet at parties usually can't. It's all about people searching for oil and assuming you have it.

Robin Swicord: The scripts I've written are my emissaries to the world, and if producers and studio executives and directors want to work with the sort of writer who's written these screenplays, I'm available. I've never consciously tried to meet people I thought would do my career some good. I'm not even sure that's how writers get hired. It's all about the work. I'm thinking of one writer who shall remain nameless, who mostly rewrites other people. He doesn't actually have original screenplays. He's the one who gets hired when the movie is already going into production and his job is to come in, walk all over the other person's script, and make something scarier or funnier. He's like a short-order cook when it comes to writing. That guy'd better go to parties because he's the type of person with whom the director wants to hang out or be on the set with for four weeks. Their personality and their ability to connect with people and schmooze are what get them the job. The bottom line is, a mediocre script will never get sold because you met someone at a party.

75. Don't Isolate Yourself, Except to Write

I like living too much to be seated all day at a desk.
—Pablo Neruda

Writing is a solitary task requiring hours of concentrated effort, and most writers should be comfortable with this solitude. Although there are some advantages to it, such as working your own hours, there are also disadvantages, like loneliness and a sense of being cut off from the outside world. Also, it can't be too healthy to sit in front of a computer screen all day. You shouldn't be afraid to go out once in a while. This would be one reason to join a writer's group, or get a part-time job in the industry.

Steven de Souza: Attending conferences can be a good idea because of the validation a beginning writer can get by interacting with other writers who will share common experiences and tips. You get encouragement by hearing other people's stories and it's an opportunity to get out of your little closet of solitude.

Michael Schiffer: I get up in the morning and leave the house to get a cup of coffee. It's always exciting to get to my desk after getting a taste of the world, just getting the light and the energy of the world inside me. As a writer, you get so cut off. You spend so many hours alone, and if you also live alone, it's even worse. I need to connect with the outside world, but not so much that I blow my focus and energy.

Tom Schulman: You can't be a hermit. A writer is an observer, someone who writes about the world, so you have to experience it. Certainly, I applaud and admire the writer who can spend many hours alone doing the work, or can go off into the woods for months at a time. But you need to balance it by getting out of your cocoon, talking to people, seeing movies, and interacting with the world.

76. Gain Value from Every Opportunity

> *It is one of the most beautiful compensations*
> *of this life that no one can sincerely try to help*
> *another without helping himself.*
> —Ralph Waldo Emerson

Since the familiar saying, "It's who you know," can be true for writers, any relationship, no matter how trivial it may seem, is a resource and a link to any opportunity. The genesis of this project is a good example. As an executive attending a pitch fest, I had the chance to help a writer I didn't know with a particular take on the story she'd just pitched me. I didn't think anything of it. She was one of a hundred writers there that day. But apparently, I'd made such a strong impression on her that she recommended me to a friend, who happened to run a major screenwriting conference, and who asked me to serve on a faculty panel. At that conference, I was introduced to a book editor who inquired about various projects I was working on. So I pitched this book's concept, and she liked it and asked me to send her the proposal, which I did, and her publisher later accepted it. Everything was a chain of events sparked by the fact that I helped an anonymous writer at a pitch conference.

Every chance meeting is an opportunity. Don't dismiss them so easily. And be nice to everyone you meet.

Steven de Souza: If I were starting out and had a choice between a high-paying job at a car dealership or a crummy-paying job that was remotely show business, I'd take the show-business job in a heartbeat. Any way to get in is smart, even if it's a nonpaying job. It's a great way to make contacts. Anybody who works at that studio will walk by your desk. You'll hear about other opportunities. I know so many people who started out as gofers somewhere, which ultimately led to assisting jobs, which led to better opportunities down the road. Anybody who complains they can't get their first break is just too narrow-minded in their definition of exactly what defines a show-business job.

Akiva Goldsman: Everyone knows someone who knows someone who knows an assistant. If your script is truly great, it'll rise to the top because there's so little great writing out there. It doesn't mean you don't have to still be ingenious when it comes to getting it seen. Everyone starts with, "Who do I know who knows somebody in Hollywood?" That's part of the job. It's how you break in. Joel [Schumacher] used to say, "If it was easy, they'd hire their relatives."

Terry Rossio: Get something produced. If nothing else, start your own Claymation company, but get some product out there. People who are creating actual product—not screenplays—are moving ahead of you every day. A student at CalArts working on a CGI [computer generated imagery] short has a better chance of gaining creative authority in Hollywood than a hundred screenwriters with a hundred screenplays. A writer has to seek out and align with the means of production, whether it's a production company, or a network, animation studio, shooting commercials, whatever. If that can't happen, the writer has to take it upon themselves to invent the means of production.

77. Have Mentors

> *Those who seek mentoring will rule the great expanse*
> *under heaven. Those who boast that they are greater*
> *than others will fall short. Those who are willing to*
> *learn from others become greater. Those who are*
> *ego-involved will be humbled and made small.*
>
> —CONFUCIUS, *SHU CHING*

The word "mentor" comes from classic Greek mythology. Mentor, a wise teacher, was asked by Odysseus to watch over his son while he embarked on a long voyage. As a surrogate parent, Mentor gave to the young child support, love, guidance, and protection. Today, we've come to know mentors as those who gently guide and nurture the growth of others. They act as teachers, counselors, and advocates who show newcomers (their protégés) the ropes, share with them their wisdom and experience, and offer insight to support their dreams. A good mentor can take years off the learning process for any aspiring writer—but not replace it. Writers still have to pay their dues. Mentors just make it a little easier.

Steven de Souza: I learned a lot from the people I was working for. They allowed me incredible access to all the different facets of film-making, like letting me into the editing room. They taught me about rewriting myself and reading my own dialogue out loud, and especially about the business of show business. I found that most of the people I've learned the most from, even though they're not writers now, started as writers.

Akiva Goldsman: I've had a bunch of them—Joel Schumacher, first and foremost. I got a meeting with Lorenzo di Bonaventura, who was then a creative executive and who had read *Indian Summer* (filmed as *Silent Fall)* and liked it, and he said, "I can't sell this to the studio, but here are some projects that have been forgotten and have no priority. Do you want to rewrite one of them?"

Some months later, I get a call from Lorenzo asking me if I had read *The Client*. They were about to start production, the script wasn't working, they were looking for someone to rewrite it, and did I want to go meet with Joel. So I read the book and I read the script, and on a Saturday, I went to Joel's house and we had a conversation. We just talked about life and the book, and how he had read *Indian Summer* and quite liked it. As I was leaving, he said it would be really fun to do this together, and I was thinking, "Well, this didn't work out."

So I went home. I didn't have a car phone, and there were six messages on my machine [at home]. I'm about to play the messages when my phone rings again and it's Lorenzo saying, "Congratulations, you've got the job. You've got to meet Joel at his house tomorrow morning."

So I finished *The Client* and went directly to the set of *Indian Summer*.

And then Joel calls me up and says, "The script for *Batman Forever* isn't working . . ." And so it went.

Amy Holden Jones: Martin Scorsese was the first person to help me into the industry after I won a film festival where he was a judge. I wish I had a mentor as a writer, but I've mentored other writers extensively. Some have done extremely well and others have not. Generally, the difference has to do with how much they persevere, how critical they are of their work, how able they are to pick themselves up from a large amount of failure and keep going, and how realistic their plan is for getting ahead in the movies. But the single biggest contributing factor is whether they're able to write—not just a great script, but a script I'd define as "a movie," which is a very narrow range of things.

Laeta Kalogridis: I took an independent study from Dan Pyne at UCLA, and he mentored me in the writing of my Joan of Arc script. His advice was not "Write what you know" but "Write what you love." Best advice I ever got.

Jim Kouf: A sort-of mentor was Dorothea Petrie, who really got me to focus on rewriting. For very little money, she got me to rewrite and rewrite and rewrite. And I think that was the most valuable lesson I ever learned as a writer, the value of rewriting, to be able to go over your work again and again and again.

Terry Rossio: I certainly learned a lot working with Ron Clements and John Musker on *Aladdin*, and from Jeffrey Katzenberg. In animation, you're in the room with talented folk every day, and you can't help but learn.

Eric Roth: There are a couple of people whose work I respect a lot, who were kind of a mentor to me and took a particular interest in me and gave me advice, mainly in maintaining a high standard of quality. But most of the advice came from people I worked for, especially directors.

Tom Schulman: My only mentors were the screenplays of the great writers I read when I started out—Robert Riskin, Paddy Chayefsky, and Billy Wilder.

CHAPTER 17

GETTING AN AGENT

78. Get the Right Agent the Old-Fashioned Way

We do not employ the writer; the writer employs us.
—LEE G. ROSENBERG

Because most writers aren't very good at selling their own scripts to producers and, more important, because having an agent validates them as professionals in the eyes of the industry, the question becomes not whether you need an agent but how do you get one?

A great script always finds an agent. Always. Guaranteed. No exceptions. It's all about money. Agents know a great script will sell in an instant, and if it doesn't, it will be a great writing sample to generate work for the talented writer. If your script isn't great yet, keep rewriting it until it is. No one wants to represent so-so material when their reputation is on the line.

Your first inclination may be the shotgun approach of writing hundreds of query letters to WGA-franchised agencies, hoping one or more will respond. Big mistake (see next habit). The consensus in the industry is that clients come to agents through referrals—someone they know, whose taste they respect, has read your script, liked it, and put their stamp of approval on it, recommending you to them. Sure, there are some isolated exceptions of writers getting represented off a query letter, so I'm not saying it's impossible (they still had a great script). What I'm saying is that 99 percent of legitimate (too busy trying to get work for their clients) agencies don't read query letters. So you've got to play the odds.

Ron Bass: It was easy for me because I was already an entertainment lawyer. So I called up a really good friend who was an agent, and said that I'd written a novel, would he take a look at it, and he said sure. I had the great luck of being in the industry already.

Steven de Souza: I got my agent through my aunt, who referred me. But I still had to have great writing samples to impress him. The only thing you can do is make your script the best that it can be, because there's no such thing as a perfect script. Every year you get all these critics listing their top ten best films of the year, and they're all different. What's best and what's not are subjective things. The perfect script is the one where you've done every possible thing you can think of that absolutely represents your best work. *That's* the perfect script.

Gerald DiPego: I attracted an agent because I had the beginning of a sale. I had optioned a screenplay just by networking on my own, then I happened to be at a gathering where I was introduced to a woman who was an agent's assistant. She asked me what I had done, and I said I just optioned a script. I guess that legitimized me because she said she'd talk to her boss.

Leslie Dixon: When you're starting out, it's best to get little agents who are just building their client lists, and are wildly enthusiastic about your work—better than the larger ones who'll never return your calls. With our first script, my friend and I split up the work: He was pounding the pavement trying to find us an agent, and I was doing all the typing. He found little tiny agencies that were barely on the map, flirted with the receptionists, anything that would get results. But I'll say this: Without an agent, you've got nothing. All your efforts once you move here should be on getting an agent. It's a validation and an umbilicus to the inside. Otherwise, you're just scrambling on the outside, looking in.

Derek Haas: It's all about a great script surrounding a big idea written in a fresh voice. A script like that glows in the dark and will find its way into the right hands.

Michael Brandt: We cheated! An Internet company wanted to hire us to write cartoons online, right when the Internet was taking off and no one knew where it was going to go as far as entertainment was concerned. We called an agent at a little agency and said we needed someone to make this deal for us. Then we slipped him our first script and said, "Oh, by the way, we also have this and a producer is interested in it." Which was true. He signed us after he read it, and we sold that script.

Jim Kouf: You have to write a good script that gets somebody's attention. Period. I'd gone to school with a friend whose father was a soundman who knew a writer who wrote a lot of TV stuff in the 1950s, and he introduced me to her. She knew what it took to make it and she said, "If you want be a writer, you've got to write something. Pick out a show on TV and write me a script for it." This was the first advice I ever received. So I did. She looked at it and said, "Okay, you can write. Now write me another one." So I went back and wrote another one. And she said, "Okay. That's good. Now write me another one." And those were the first three scripts I ever wrote. Then she said, "Okay, now let's see if we can get you an agent." So I got an agent based on those three scripts. They never sold, but they helped get me started.

As to my first deal, I started in show business at the same time a friend of mine started, but he wanted to be a producer, so he eventually wound up at ICM. He introduced me to Dan Petrie Jr., who at the time was also in the mailroom, going to be an agent, and he optioned my script to his mother, Dorothea Petrie, who was a producer. So my first deal as a writer was his first deal as an agent.

Bill Marsilii: People often say, "Write a great script," and you just want to shrug and say, "I know this, but what's the real secret?" It's difficult because I know several writers who wrote very good, very producible screenplays and still can't get any representation. So I don't think it's fair to just say write a great screenplay. While I don't think there is one single thing one can do, I believe that there are several things one can do, which after a while greatly increase your chances. For instance, if you choose a very strong idea for your screenplay, preferably in a popular genre, if you write roles that are actor bait, if you write a great opening, you increase your chances exponentially.

Another helpful tip is to think of your screenplay as a writing sample, not something you will sell right off the bat. Focus on writing the kinds of stories you love, the kinds of movies you want to write in the future, and on showcasing your talents on the page. In my case, I had a good friend who was a reader at MGM, so I asked him as a favor if he'd be willing to read my script just to know how it would stack up against the stuff he was reading every day. After he read it, he called me up and said, "This is better than 99 percent of the stuff my bosses hand me. Can I show it to them?" Now, it didn't sell, but when the execs found out I was unrepresented, they started contacting agents on my behalf.

Scott Rosenberg: I had a very Zen approach to the whole thing because I had friends who, when they came out here, immediately did that mass mailing of query letters and no response. So I always had the attitude that when I was ready, they would find me. And it's pretty much what happened. I was constantly writing and getting better until I placed in a contest, and I had my pick of agents. Besides, you don't necessarily need a fancy agent right away. The hardest part is to go from no-agent to agent.

Terry Rossio: We got our agent through the recommendation of a producer, and that happened because the project was deemed exceptional, from concept through execution. We had a dozen screenplays prior to that we didn't send out, because we knew they weren't good enough. We were smart to not paper the town with our practice scripts. I'm of the belief a writer's entire focus should be on creating quality material, and if that can be accomplished, the agents will appear.

Eric Roth: I got my first agent as a result of winning the Samuel Goldwyn Award at UCLA.

Michael Schiffer: I got my first agent simply by sending out my best writing sample and having somebody respond to it, through a referral by a friend.

Ed Solomon: I hate to say this, but if your script is genuinely good it will attract agents like a magnet. The sad truth is that most scripts aren't that good.

Robin Swicord: I put up a play with some friends, and an agent happened to see it and asked to represent me. She is still my agent to this day. If you're starting out, I'd recommend you get the agent that loves your work over the one who says, "I think I can sell this and I could probably get you some meetings." You want the agent who says, "You're so great, I'm gonna give you such a career!" I'm very lucky that I like my agent, that we can call her as I'd call a family member.

Agents can be very destructive to writers and totally erode their confidence. Often, they represent you because they feel they can sell a project, and when it doesn't sell, they forget about you. You want someone who'll travel the long road by your side and who's hungry enough. The agent with the big office and three assistants will not read your script, but their assistant, who'll be an agent one day, will be hungry enough to read it. So it's very important to choose the person that really loves your writing.

79. Never Write a Query Letter Again

There are no rules, but you break them at your peril.
—ANONYMOUS

Of all the habits explored in this book, this will probably generate the most debate, because for the past thirty years it's been the most given advice in conferences, blogs, magazines, and books. But my personal experience and that of my colleagues in the trenches of the industry disproves it. As you've seen, only one of our twenty-two mentors got an agent or sold a script because a producer responded to a query letter, and this was a year later.

The reality is that no *legitimate*—therefore overworked—executive, producer, agent, assistant, or manager reads them. If you worked sixteen-hour days, making and returning over a hundred phone calls, taking meetings and lunches, attending screenings, staff meetings, negotiations, and functions, being pulled in several directions by demands from bosses, clients, clients' managers, other agents, producers, development executives, and lawyers, and then spent your entire weekend reading ten to thirty scripts, while trying to have a personal life, would you spend even one rare minute reading a letter from an unknown writer? Probably not. So save your energy to write the best script you can, one that'll impress anyone who'll then recommend it to a producer or agent they know. In Hollywood, a referral from a known and respected source will always have more clout than a query from a stranger.

Jim Kouf: I get a lot of query letters. Is this a new thing? Is this what the books and seminars tell you to do? Because nobody reads them. I certainly don't. I literally don't have the time to sit down and read them. If you really want to be a screenwriter, you've got to get in there and be there with the people. You have to get a job on the set, meet producers, directors, actors, assistants. You can't do it through the mail.

Here's how it works: My ex-brother-in-law, who's a fireman, calls me and he has a fireman friend who's written a script. So he asks me whether I'd read the script, and I say, "For you, as a favor, sure, I'll read it." So I take the script and I read the first few pages and I say, "Okay, it's well written enough." But I don't have time to read the whole thing, so I send it to the agency, and they read it and they like it, and now I'm trying to see if my agent wants to handle this guy. All because of my ex-brother-in-law, and a great script. That's how it happens.

CHAPTER 18

PITCHING

80. Believe in Your Work

Some of the world's greatest feats were accomplished by
people not smart enough to know they were impossible.
—DOUG LARSON

Hollywood is full of stories about projects that took years to sell because the writers or producers believed in them, never taking "no" as a final answer. You *must* believe in your story, because a studio only worries about selling the movie in seconds, whether it's sixty seconds in a trailer, or ten seconds with a newspaper ad or poster. You have to adopt the attitude that you've got the best movie they'll ever hear, and they're lucky to be given the opportunity to hear it.

Gerald DiPego: That inner love of your story is an important measuring stick. If it makes you laugh, if it makes you cry, if it touches you in some deep way, then you've got to trust there are other people out there who'll feel the same. You may have to go through a hundred [readers] before you get to the one who'll feel that way, but it's important to hold on to that.

Ed Solomon: The most important thing in preparing for a pitch is believing in the material. Your belief in it and your ability to lean on the story, *not* your reliance on pizzazz, flash, or hook, are the key elements. If you're telling a good story, you naturally have a hook.

81. Rehearse Your Pitch until It's Flawless

Life's a pitch!
—DAVID DWORSKI

Since pitching is a verbal presentation, and therefore a performance, rehearsing it is a common habit among working screenwriters. Every chance they get, they pitch their story to friends and family, to their pets even, so that it flows naturally. They pay close attention to what parts in the story people respond to, and what questions they ask when certain parts are unclear, allowing them to embellish and rehearse the story until it's a good yarn.

Ron Bass: Preparing is very time consuming. When I started out, going around trying to get jobs, I had six to eight stories all worked out. I never write anything down because then it becomes too mechanical. So I say it to myself over and over many times, developing it as a sort of speech, pacing around alone until I get it the way I like it. I repeat it often enough until it reaches a point where it's not completely memorized, but close, where I can say it so casually that it doesn't sound memorized, more like I'm speaking fluidly.

Gerald DiPego: Pitching is a skill you need to learn. I prepare for it by trying to distill the idea into its essence, making it exciting and clear and finding ways to put my enthusiasm into the storytelling. I pitch it to myself a couple of times, then I pitch it to my wife, which really helps because the first few pitches will be awkward.

Derek Haas: Know the story and practice it. We always practice our pitches before we do them. We write them out in detail, then get together and practice our asses off until we know the story backward and forward. We keep it to under fifteen minutes and tell the entire story of the movie. A good trick is to talk about the characters ahead of time—"Before we start the pitch, we want to just talk about the characters for a second." Then it doesn't seem like we're already pitching, even though we are. Also, once the pitch begins, you can now speak shorthand about the characters.

Amy Holden Jones: It's useful to start telling the story to your friends in thirty seconds first, then in five minutes. Pay attention to the first times they get distracted. If their eyes glaze over, you have a problem. If you keep telling the story and refining it until you can tell from your audience that it's worth pursuing, you'll have a complete story with interesting characters. If you never reach this point, you'll probably have a story that'll never interest anyone.

82. Know the Story Inside and Out Without Rehearsing

When it comes to preparing for a pitch, there are just as many screenwriters who don't rehearse the story for fear of losing spontaneity and enthusiasm in the room. Rehearsed or not, they're always prepared by knowing the story inside and out. The most important thing is to keep the bored executive from falling asleep, and engage his or her imagination and interest.

Akiva Goldsman: I don't rehearse, but you certainly need to know your story well before you can pitch it. I'm lucky that I'm social, because it's true that pitching is a social art. Relationships are irrelevant, because you can go into a room with someone you have a relationship with and not sell it. To all the introvert writers who have a tough time pitching, my advice is to not worry about pitching. Concentrate on the writing, because you won't get to pitch unless you've written well in the first place. If you're lucky and get called in to pitch, get a best friend or producer who'll help you practice. You don't have to be a great pitcher if you're a great writer. I know brilliant writers who are terrible in the room.

Aline Brosh McKenna: I try not to rehearse too much because I want to keep it fresh. If it's been rehearsed too much, or it sounds like a scripted thing, it loses its freshness. If it becomes too boring for you, it'll be boring for them.

Scott Rosenberg: I don't rehearse it consciously, but the thing about me is that when I get an idea that really excites me, I love pitching it to my friends.

Eric Roth: I don't pitch very well, so I do it as infrequently as I can. I don't bother to prepare, but I'll come in knowing what the material is about, even though I may not know the story per se. I'll say, this is an area I'm interested in, these are the people that are involved; then I'll give them a sense of what the movie could be like, the general tone, and main values. And I've been fairly successful, so they know I can always back up what I have to say with my material.

Tom Schulman: My way of preparing for a pitch is, unfortunately, to write the story. A lot of people make the mistake of thinking they can go in and pitch their story in general terms, whether it's because they haven't worked out the story, or because of the sheer commerciality of the idea that they think someone will buy it on the spot. The reality is that most executives want to know the whole thing. It's like sitting around the campfire, saying, "Once upon a time . . ." and getting the people involved in your story so that they can't wait to hear what'll happen next or what'll happen to the main character. The story controls the room. If it's interesting and you're excited about it, your enthusiasm will come through. If you have doubts and problems with it, it'll also show through. Once the story is written, I'm prepared. I don't really rehearse it. I just go in and tell them the story. But I find that when you talk about your story to other writers as you're developing it, you can sense where your weaknesses are by their reactions to it.

83. Keep the Pitch Short, Simple, and Exciting

> *It never gets better than the romance and the blush.*
> —SYD FIELD

Because pitching is a performance, it should be viewed as an emotional and mental seduction of a listener. And because the listener is most often an overworked and stressed-out executive with a short attention span, the key is to keep your story as short and simple as possible, while still communicating the passion of the story with energy, enthusiasm, and excitement. Matching the pitch to the genre also helps. If it's a thriller, make it thrilling and suspenseful, and keep the listener riveted. If it's a comedy, make it fun.

Ron Bass: Since you only have a short amount of time to tell your story, you only stress the key elements of the story—the entertaining, interesting parts. It's a performance. It should be engrossing, compelling, and exciting.

Steven de Souza: I pitch off my three-by-five cards, because if I go deeper I have too much detail. You need to keep it simple and short, and you've got to be entertaining. But if you're starting out, it's probably better to spend your time writing than pitching, because nine times out of ten, if a studio buys your pitch, they'll get rid of you and hire a more established writer to write the script. They don't want to waste time on an untried writer and have to wait twelve weeks to know something they already know, which is that they'll get rid of you anyway. I can't tell you how many times I've been hired to write a script based on a pitch by a first-time writer. The writer pitches, the studio tells him to go write an outline, he or she comes back with five typed pages, the studio says, "Thank you very much," and they hire me because they know I can deliver an acceptable script in twelve weeks. So if you really want to write the story, it's a risky proposition to pitch it. You're better off spending the extra time writing the script.

Leslie Dixon: Be enthusiastic, make it short, and most important, don't be desperate. They'll either sense it's a movie or not. It helps to have more material prepared than you actually present, so if they ask questions like, "What happens here?" you can answer them.

Aline Brosh McKenna: I try to look at it as not pitching but as going in and trying to tell a good yarn at a dinner party, and try make it as conversational as possible. I still go in knowing my story and having an outline to refer to, but I don't have a performance approach to it. I just tell the key points of the story, because you can always fill in if someone asks you a question. The rookie mistake is to always say too much.

Scott Rosenberg: You have to know what to pitch and who to pitch to. In terms of what to pitch, I'd never pitch *Beautiful Girls*, but I could pitch *Con Air* in fifteen seconds. The key to a good pitch is trying to do it in under five minutes. Know what to leave in and what to leave out. Also, have the answers to every question they may have. You may not have said it but you know it, so you allow them to have this question-and-answer session, and if you can answer all the questions and be done with the pitch in five minutes, you're golden.

Executives want to know the act delineations—the general beginning, middle, and end of the story, and they want to know your characters. It's important to let them know where they are in the script because you could've been going on for twenty minutes and yet, you're only on page twenty. When you finish pitching the story, they should be able to see the poster.

They need to quickly see the movie in their heads because all they're thinking about is how they're going to sell the movie. If they can see it and it's exciting, they'll buy the pitch. Another tip: I always cast my characters so executives can see them right there. So instead of "Fred and Bob duke it out," it's "Nick Cage and Kevin Spacey duke it out." It makes it easier for them to visualize and follow the story better.

Terry Rossio: We live in a world now of props—show and tell. For our last project, I spent nearly $30,000 creating a sizzle reel. The producers told me later that's what sold them on the project. Whether it's a graphic novel or an animatic or a proof-of-concept short film or a visual development board, I don't walk in the door empty-handed.

Ed Solomon: Genuine interest in what you're pitching is by far the best thing. Being able to tell your story in extremely short, short, medium, and lengthy versions is also important. You need to have several versions prepared, so that if you need to, you can tell what your story is about in thirty seconds, in three minutes, or in twenty minutes.

84. Overcome Nervousness and Don't Show Desperation

Fear cannot be banished, but it can be calm and without panic; and it can be mitigated by reason and evaluation.

—Vannevar Bush

If being dull is sin number one in Hollywood, then showing desperation is sin number two. It's like that old commercial advises, "Never let them see you sweat." Chances are you're not nervous when you talk enthusiastically to your friends or loved ones about a great film you just saw.

A film teacher used to teach his students how to pitch by having them pitch their favorite film, to show that when you're excited about a story and familiar with it (assuming they've seen it multiple times), telling the story with enthusiasm is a natural act. Pitching, like telling your friends about a good movie, is simply about sharing the high points of a story to get someone excited enough to see it.

Sure, there may be more at stake: Writer Bo Zenga calls it the "Two-by-Four Theory." If you put a two-by-four on two cinder blocks and ask someone to walk across it, no problem. But if you put the same two-by-four across two buildings, it's a different story. Same two-by-four, same distance to cross, but the stakes are higher.

If you're nervous, tell the executive. Don't hide it, or you'll lose the energy you need to think about your story. Have fun! Enter the room with the right attitude. Nothing succeeds in Hollywood like the appearance of success. You have to believe you have the upper hand, that the executive is the lucky one for getting to hear your incredible story, not the other way around, where you go in like a sacrificial lamb and grovel because they gave you an opportunity to tell them your story. The bottom line is that they need material to survive and you're their main supplier with lots of buyers to choose from. In other words, they need *you*.

Ron Bass: Not memorizing your pitch is important, because if you fumble or get confused and have to make unexpected decisions during the pitch, you'll look very uncertain. The way you present yourself has a lot to do with how much the buyer has confidence that you'll be able to write what you're pitching.

Gerald DiPego: Once you're in the room, you'll be nervous. You need to take a breath and take the focus off the room. It helps if you're in love with the story, because your enthusiasm and passion will help sell it. It's a challenge if you're shy. You hope they'll give their undivided attention, that they won't take phone calls, or that the secretary won't come in the middle. You have to be prepared, and not be thrown by that.

Leslie Dixon: You just have to know what you're doing. It helps if you have an entertaining personality. Most of the writers I know in this town have big personalities. I think the bigger your personality, the more of a tool you have, and a very strong voice will come into your writing. Pitching is basically sitting in a room and talking.

Laeta Kalogridis: Be prepared, but stay loose. Respond to the people in the room, not your prewritten outline or cards.

Andrew W. Marlowe: The first time you do anything in front of someone, you'll be nervous. But if you do it enough times, you'll get more comfortable at it. The only way to get over nervousness is to practice. Tell your story to a friend, so that when you finally get in the room, it's not the first time it's coming out of your mouth. And tell the story as if you're sitting around a campfire, and you're trying to get them emotionally engaged. You're telling them the story as if you've just seen the movie the night before and it's your favorite movie ever.

Terry Rossio: Regarding nerves, my technique is to tell the basic story quickly, in about six minutes. Then let the studio or the producers ask questions. That gets them involved, and creates a give-and-take.

Michael Schiffer: I view a pitch meeting as a creative process, much like a story meeting, an opportunity to share my story with someone who'll comment on it and maybe make it better. So I'll sometimes take notes of what's said to me during the pitch. I'll even interrupt my pitch to write things I haven't thought of before if it would make the story better. Executives are filmmakers too. They hear a million pitches and they usually have good instincts. They'll probably even be your editor in the development process, throwing story ideas along the way, so don't be shocked if it starts at the pitch meeting. In fact, that's a good sign. If they sit there and have nothing to say, either you've hit a grand-slam home run or you've bombed.

Ed Solomon: What's important is taking a moment to focus and think of your pitch as a performance in the same way an actor or a musician would. Focus before you go in and think about what you're trying to get across. If you're good enough, you can certainly sell crap and pretend it's good, but that's a much lower-odds game than if your story is really good and you believe in it. I've also found that not needing to sell it is one of the best ways *to* sell it. Quiet confidence that what you have is of value is far more persuasive than the need to sell it. Explaining to someone why they'd like what you have to offer only insults them more, because they know their business better than you. At the very least, they know whether it's a movie or not, and if they can make money off it. Also, remember that you're communicating several things at once: your story—it must be interesting—and who *you* are; that's an equally important part.

85. Adapt to Any Situation

> *Question: How many development executives does it take to change a light bulb? Answer: Does it have to be a light bulb?*
> —OLD INDUSTRY JOKE

You shouldn't be unnerved by interruptions and often by mind-blowing suggestions from executives about how to make your story more commercial. Executives' phones never stop ringing, and it's always a good sign when they instruct their assistants to hold their calls. But just because the executive you're pitching to takes a call, it doesn't mean your pitch is dead in the water (although it could: some executives work out a system where they get their assistant to interrupt pitches of absolutely no interest).

Because you never know what to expect, you need to be flexible, adjust to any unusual circumstance in the room, and be prepared to pick up where you left off.

Michael Schiffer: Don't have a canned pitch, because you can always count on being interrupted by an "important" phone call. You want to be talking to a human being. Your pitch will vary according to the executive's body language, their facial signals, how fast or slow to go, if they're following you, or if their eyes glaze over. And they'll ask you questions in the middle of your pitch, so you have to know where to pick up again. If a canned pitch worked, you might as well tape it and send it around town.

I had a pitch meeting once, where I thought I had someone in the palm of my hand, until she got a phone call in the middle of the meeting, and then my pitch turned to ashes. I didn't understand what happened. Later, I found out that in the middle of my pitch, she had gotten fired. When she returned to the office, she just sat through the rest of my pitch without saying anything, while I was fumbling. In that case, I wished I was on tape.

Tom Schulman: I've had just about everything you could imagine go wrong at a pitch meeting, like starting with, "This is a story about a fifty-year-old guy," and within seconds, the executive interrupts with, "Could it be a seventy-year-old guy?" and you go, "Well, let me go on with the story." And they go, "Why couldn't he be seventy?" because, unbeknownst to you, they've just signed a deal with Jack Nicholson, and they're trying to squeeze him into your story. Or they try to change the gender of your main character, or the executive seems absolutely distracted by everything in the room except your story, and then you're surprised when they buy it. Or the opposite, where you're just on a roll, and they're riveted, and they give you great ideas on the story, but they're just not interested.

Ed Solomon: It's not as important to have the perfect pitch memorized because frankly anything can throw it off—a phone call in the middle of it, someone asking a question, another only wanting to hear parts of it. What's more important is knowing what your story is about and having the confidence that it's the real thing.

CHAPTER 19

ACTING LIKE A PROFESSIONAL

86. Don't Be Paranoid about Your Ideas Being Stolen

It used to be that executives could spot an amateur by the look of his or her script—the page count, the number and quality of brads used, or whether a WGA registration number, draft number, or date were printed on the cover page. Now, it's the instant a writer says, "How do I know you won't steal my idea?"

Why? Because it's a useless worry for something that rarely happens in legitimate circles. There are two important reasons why executives almost never steal ideas (it's still possible, but very rare). One is financial. It costs a lot less to buy an idea from a beginning writer than to fight a lawsuit in court. The other is interpersonal. Because relationships and appearances are crucial to executives, they won't risk embarrassment and losing their jobs should they be faced with a lawsuit. It's just not worth it. This is why executives are so careful to avoid even the slightest potential for a lawsuit by avoiding reading unsolicited material, and making sure that release forms of all kinds are signed, or that submissions come through legitimate channels, like agents, attorneys, or people they absolutely trust.

A common scenario is of the paranoid writer who never lets go of his "original" idea, only to read in the trades that another writer has just sold the very same idea. "How could it be? I've never told anyone about it," claims the shocked amateur. It's the universal consciousness. As soon as you think up an idea, at least four other people around the world come up with the exact one. What's important in Hollywood isn't just the idea, but the unique execution of the idea that the writer brings to the table. So if you think you have such a unique idea (doubtful, but possible), develop it into an outline or script. Otherwise, relax and free your energies for other worthwhile habits. Professional screenwriters, who also have attorneys and agents, protect their developed work by registering it with the WGA [Writers Guild of America] or U.S. Copyright Office, and they keep detailed records and logs of phone calls, meetings, business lunches, and memos.

Ron Bass: [Stealing my ideas is] something I've never worried about, maybe because I used to be an entertainment lawyer, and you know that in legitimate circles, it just doesn't happen, in general. It's relatively rare when someone feels that the best thing for them to do is steal your idea. I'm sure it can happen, and has happened, but you can't really function in the business worrying about it.

Derek Haas: I don't think you should be paranoid about ideas being stolen. I mean, we literally had our first idea taken by a producer, but we found there's little you can do about it. Ideas aren't copyrightable. So quit worrying; they won't hire you for your idea but for how you execute that idea.

Michael Brandt: To me that's the biggest rookie move there is, and the surest way to never make it in this town. You gotta put yourself and your ideas out there. Or you can just take your ideas back to Kansas with you, and rest assured that no one would ever take them from you. That's one less writer we have to worry about.

Laeta Kalogridis: Ideas are seldom as valuable as execution, so one shouldn't worry about them being stolen. You can have the greatest idea in the world, and it isn't worth anything if you can't execute it. Also, there are very few ideas that are really revolutionary in themselves.

Michael Schiffer: Most professionals in the business will bend over backward to avoid even the slightest impression that they've borrowed your idea. The last thing they want to hear is anything remotely close to what they're developing, so they'll stop you. On the other hand, nonlegitimate and desperate people who hear your idea at a coffee shop could run out and sell it, so be cautious in public.

87. Don't Pitch in Social Situations

Talking about an idea squeezes the juice out of it.
—Ernest Hemingway

Generally, you shouldn't worry about pitching, because you won't even get a chance to pitch unless you've either sold a script or made a profitable movie. But even if you happen to meet an executive at a social function, your first inclination shouldn't be to pitch your ideas. Executives constantly get blitzed by unsolicited material—valets leaving scripts on their car seat, people pitching to them at weddings, bar mitzvahs, in restaurant bathrooms, you name it. When they meet you, the last thing they want is to hear another idea. In fact, it's such a typical occurrence that they probably will be dreading that you'll launch into one at any moment.

Screenwriter Les Bohem calls this the "Nashville handshake"—no one ever shakes hands in Nashville without putting a demo tape in your hands. But if they're genuinely interested, and ask what you've done or are currently working on, then by all means, do tell. Otherwise, don't be afraid to ask for an official meeting, and say you'll have your agent or attorney set it up. This will make a more favorable impression.

Jim Kouf: Nobody wants to go to a party and listen to somebody's idea. This usually happens from someone who has no other access to them, so they're immediately considered an amateur. Professional writers set it up through normal channels, like an agent or attorney. That's the way to do it.

Eric Roth: You only do it if someone asks you what you're working on and wants to hear what your story is about. Otherwise, no one wants to talk business in social situations.

Michael Schiffer: We're constantly cranking out stories, working on characters and plots, and my rule is, when I leave my office, to think about being alive in the world. I don't want to think business outside business hours. If an executive wants to hear your pitch, they'll give you signals and ask for it. But pitches out of context become triply boring because you're imposing characters and settings on someone who's usually not in the mood.

88. Don't Work for Free

There are a lot of hustlers in Hollywood who call themselves producers even if they have never produced a single thing in their lives, except business cards with the title "Producer." Since they don't have development deals, they don't have the inclination to pay writers to write scripts for them, especially when so many writers are willing to do it for free in order to break in.

The general consensus among professionals is that if these so-called "producers" can't pay you even a little money, they're not in a position to get anything made, or they don't value your work enough. First, you're risking spending months out of your life for something that may never get made. Second, chances are you won't own the material anyway. Bottom line: if a producer values your work, he or she should put some money on the line. If you still want to do business with a producer who can't pay you, write the script on spec, and then let the producer decide whether to option it.

Ron Bass: It's fine to work for free for yourself when you write on spec. First, working for free is in violation of the WGA. Even if you're not a Guild member, there's still a good reason why [the rule] exists. Its principles are the same. If someone doesn't want to pay you anything for your work, chances are this isn't a good person to be working for, and it's not a legitimate situation that'll result in something good for the writer. Then, you could end up with a conflict over who owns the work, and the other person claiming you couldn't use it. If you're willing to write it speculatively, just tell the producer you're writing it for yourself, and you'll show it to them when it's done. If they like it, they can make you an offer for what they think it's worth. If not, you can always go somewhere else with it. At least you'll own it.

Laeta Kalogridis: It's totally dependent on the producer in question. In general, [working for free] is a bad idea. You will not be valued if you don't value yourself; the idea of putting in sweat equity is too often not respected here.

Eric Roth: If the producer and the writer are both out of college and starting out, I don't think there's anything wrong with a hand-shake agreement. But if a producer *hires* you, then you shouldn't do it for free. In that case, you should sign a partner agreement with the producer so that you equally split any future rewards, which means in a sense you're writing a spec script. Never give the work away for free. No one takes a writer seriously if he's doing things for free. It's not professional. There's a sense that you're getting less.

Tom Schulman: When I started out, before I was in the Guild and had any hope of selling anything, I'd meet a lot of aspiring produc-ers, but I always got them to pay me something. Even if it was a small token, like a small option on a script, it got them motivated because they had something invested in the project.

89. Don't Be Difficult to Work With

*The greatest lesson in life is to know that even
fools are right sometimes.*
—Winston Churchill

If you're the kind of writer who would argue with executives for forty-five minutes over the color of a minor character's dress, don't be sur-prised if you find yourself labeled "difficult." Most executives, produc-ers, and directors don't like working with difficult writers for obvious reasons.

Of course, if you believe in something strongly enough, and it isn't as trivial as the color of a dress, then by all means, you should voice your opinions. One extreme is thinking your script is perfect, and notes are just a waste of time. The other is taking everything an executive says verbatim like a secretary. The ideal attitude is some-where in between. The best trick in dealing with studio notes is to lis-ten, then say, "There are some interesting ideas here. Let me explore some of them." Then, you thank them for their valuable insights and leave the room.

Ron Bass: I've walked out of many projects before, but it's not like, "I'm out of here!" in a storm of fury. You talk with the executive or the director about what they don't like and what you're doing, and you say to them, "I agree, this is the time to bring in someone else, because I don't think I'm the guy that can make it work. I don't know how to make it work." You have to understand this other person, your boss, is only saying the same thing you're saying. They have to make the same movie to their vision, and they think you're wrong. Sure, I've been in millions of arguments and screaming matches over specific scenes, but ultimately, when it comes to parting company, that person isn't getting rid of you because they don't like you. They just have a different vision they don't think you can match. Maybe you like their way and try to do it their way, but they don't think you did a good job. What else can they do but get someone else?

Michael Brandt: We like to collaborate, and notes are just another form of collaboration. You have to be able to articulate your position on why you did something the way you did it, but you also have to be willing to adapt. The best idea should win. If you hear the same note over and over, then something is probably wrong with that part of the script and you should listen.

Derek Haas: Also, while a note may seem wrong, it's often an indication there's a problem somewhere that needs addressing, and that's when you have to get into the reasoning behind the note.

Gerald DiPego: As writers in the development process, we constantly need to be on the alert to fend off bad ideas that people don't realize would hurt the material. At the same time, we have to stay open enough to embrace the good ideas. That's a real challenge. It's a whole other skill from writing. If you're the type of person who gets mad quickly, starts yelling, throws a script across the room, and walks out of a meeting (anyone can be pushed to that point), you won't last too long. Generally, it really pays to be a good listener and to consider thoughtfully what comes at you. Even if you think it's really stupid, and it might be, politely explain why it won't work.

Leslie Dixon: Do really good work. Be self-critical and make changes they don't expect you to make. If you can take their notes in your own way, you'll both be happy. If a director gets on the project, try to understand the director and become someone he or she likes to deal with. If you don't like the notes, or you're defensive and arrogant about taking them, you're not going to last. You have to figure out a way to make them feel you're working with them. They're paying you. If you realize the project is becoming the movie you didn't want to make, and you don't think it'll work, it's perfectly okay to walk away. I've done it.

Tony Gilroy: It depends on who gives you notes. I'm always looking to trade up. If a note is a good one and it makes the story better, great. But when it's a bad note, how I handle it depends on its source—is it coming from your lead actor or from the junior exec on a project I don't give a damn about? If the note is bad but important and it's coming from a powerful source and that person can't be fooled or worked around, I'd write very long e-mails and letters to them, laying out chapter and verse, putting up the whole chalkboard, laying out all the foundations, all the underpinnings, all the consequences of what they're talking about, and making a complicated and very deep case about what they're proposing, which shows them that I've seriously thought about what they're saying.

Nicholas Kazan: Being cooperative doesn't mean you're a puppet. When people say to me, "I hear you're difficult," I thank them. It's a compliment because to me, being difficult means I stand up for my opinions. If they're making a mistake, I tell them so. I support it passionately and vehemently, but I don't throw things. Everyone wants to have a good time working on a project. I like to create and make things, so the people I work with generally have a good time working with me. When they say I'm difficult, it's because they ask me to make a change, and I tell them it won't work. There are some writers who will do anything they're asked, and I don't think those writers are very good. If you do what people tell you to do, you're not writing from the inside. You're writing from the outside, and it shows. You always want to have an enthusiasm for the work and the process, explain your reasons to people, and be agreeable. If you simply say, "I can try to make that change, but it'll have the following four effects that I don't think you want," they'll consider it, they'll hear you. But if you threaten people, or are unpleasant and sour, you won't work again.

Andrew W. Marlowe: When you have good collaboration with the producers, the director, and the actors, they can push to make the content better. The worst collaborations tend to come when there are clashes of ego, [people] dealing with insecurity and trying to prove themselves. At some point you have to realize we're only talking about ink on paper. They're talking about what's on the page, not about you or your identity. They're talking about a story that anybody could make better. The collaborative process can be great if you have open and generous partners who are looking to challenge the material in the best possible way and make everybody better at what they do.

Michael Schiffer: We all lose control of our work sometimes. The key is to be open-minded. If I've structured the story, told it really well, and have it locked down, even if they bring in another writer, in many ways, all they're doing is changing the color of the curtains. They can change the dialogue here and there, they can change a few jokes, but the architecture of the piece is exactly the same. So when the director comes in, all he does is the interior decoration of the monument you've built, and that's all right. Sure, it sucks. You want to say, "Why don't you let me change it from blue to green, I can do that." But often they don't want you to, because people like to work with associates they've come to trust over many years or projects. Ultimately, it doesn't matter, because when the movie comes out, it's not the color of the curtains that dazzle people, it's the story and the character conflicts, and if you're the original author and get it right and bulletproof, it's very hard for people to mess it up.

Ed Solomon: You have to choose your battles. As a screenwriter, you're never in a position to win a fight. You can only argue your position. And it's true that "difficult" writers often get fired, unless they're really good. But if they're really this good, people don't tend to argue with them that much, because they respect their opinions. If they pay you money to write for them, they view you in the same way you view someone you hire to design a kitchen. I'm not saying I like it, but that's the way it is. I've taken stances where I've argued successfully and other times, I've been fired for it. I think the position of the screenwriter in the industry, that they're perceived as expendable and fired so easily, is detrimental to the quality of film.

90. Don't Burn Bridges When You're Fired

Getting fired from a project is common, even among highly successful screenwriters. What's also common is being rehired to fix your script after others have failed to make it better. So always be nice to your employer, even if your first instinct is to slash their Porsche's tires or burn their Malibu cottage. Understand that when you get fired, it's usually because of the work. It's not personal, even if it seems like it.

Remember Habit 57 about being open to criticism? It's tough to disassociate yourself from your material. If you get fired, you can't help but be hurt by it. It's okay to be angry. Just be professional, put on a fake smile, go home, and *then* cry or throw things. Chances are you'll get rehired on the project when the twelve rewriters they'll hire won't even get close to the magic you wove in the original draft that made them buy it in the first place. And even if they don't rehire you on this project, it's such a small town, chances are they'll consider you for future assignments.

Ron Bass: Not burning bridges is always a healthy attitude to adopt in anything in life, as long as it's not a euphemism for not being true to yourself. If you're in a situation when you feel you have to end a relationship because of the way you've been treated, you won't feel right if you don't. But that aside, and I don't think that happens a lot in our business, you want to know that even if an experience went badly, if you've decided you want to work with that person again, you'll be glad that you haven't burned the bridge, especially when getting rehired on the same project is common.

But I have yet to be fired off a project for a personal reason. You're taken off a project because somebody feels that right now, they need someone else's writing on it that you weren't able, or willing, to deliver. It's really about the work, not me personally. Sure, you're disappointed and hurt, and you wish you could still be on the project. But unless the person has been abusive to you, being furious at the person who felt you weren't doing the job is a foolish and misguided emotion in most circumstances.

Gerald DiPego: It depends on how you've been treated personally. If you feel you've been really abused by someone, you'll probably not want to work with them again. I'm not for yelling and screaming, but sometimes it's really important to clear the air and tell them how you feel, and if they've done wrong by you, tell them why you think that's wrong. So you're not exactly burning bridges, but you're not just shrugging and walking away either. Everyone knows how writers are treated in Hollywood. If writers are fired off a project for what is no good reason but just someone's whim or an insecurity, or this trend that any writer will do and of getting a fresh look from someone else, it's important for writers to go on record that this is not a good way to make movies, and that there is such a thing as a writer's vision.

Directors would never allow this to happen to them. It would be outrageous for a director to be replaced once he hands in his cut. I'd love to see what they'd think when someone says to them, "Don't take this personally, we're just bringing in another director for a fresh look, maybe a little reshooting." They'd go through the roof, and yet that's exactly what they do to writers.

Amy Holden Jones: The thing about rejection is that you should never make the people who reject you feel particularly guilty about it. Often, when they move on from you to someone who doesn't work out, if you haven't made them feel guilty, it leaves the door open for them to bring you back.

Jim Kouf: You never know when you'll work with these people again, so it's a good habit to cultivate. I had more of a temper when I was younger, but it was never about the people I was working with—more like the project. I've always stayed on pretty good terms with everybody because it's a small business, and more than likely you'll run across the same people again.

• • •

The journey to screenwriting success is full of obstacles and disappointments. If writing a quality script out of nothing weren't difficult enough, trying to market it may seem like an impossible task when faced with constant rejection. To keep the dream alive, in addition to thickening the layers of emotional skin, you need to adopt the four P's: Patience, Perseverance, Passion, and Practice.

PART 6

THE FOUR PS

Patience, Perseverance, Passion, and Practice

Nothing in the world can take the place of persistence. Talent will not; nothing is more common than unsuccessful men with talent. Genius will not; unrewarded genius is almost a proverb. Education will not; the world is full of educated derelicts. Persistence and determination alone are omnipotent.

—CALVIN COOLIDGE

CHAPTER 20

PATIENCE

91. Play the Waiting Game

Everything comes to him who hustles while he waits.
—THOMAS EDISON

A screenwriter's life in Hollywood is a long waiting game—between handing a draft to your agent and getting feedback, between pitching and decision, or between dealing with attorneys and finally getting paid. Even when a project gets green-lighted, it can take over a year and a half from preproduction to wide release. You need patience and you need to pace yourself.

At first, a lot of people act in desperation out of impatience and a need to succeed. Don't be angry or discouraged if it takes an agent, producer, or development executive a long time to respond to your script. Some say you should give them two weeks. The reality is more like two months. It's just a matter of priorities. A "hot" spec up for a bidding war will get read over a lunch hour, whereas reading a "recommended" script from an unknown writer will depend on the relationship between producer and agent.

Steven de Souza: Be patient, keep your fingers crossed, and believe your ideas are viable and valuable. Though studios don't want what you just wrote this week, the tide can turn on a dime. Michael Crichton told me he had the script for *ER* in his drawer for eighteen years! He wrote that script as a pilot for a network series but had the dumb luck of turning it in right after a movie of his flopped. Unable to come to a decision based on the merits of the script, the network executive decided to pass. So Michael kept this script in a drawer and concentrated on his novels and big movies. Then he heard that Spielberg was looking for a medical show, so he took the script out of the filing cabinet and thought he'd have to rewrite it. But to his surprise, he only had to update the equipment and technical jargon.

Akiva Goldsman: It's very hard to be patient because you put so much energy into something. It's your first priority for so long, but it's someone else's two-hundredth priority. That's painful. You have to have wisdom, empathy, and understanding. Also, don't waste your energy staring at the phone. I'm speaking from experience. You get into this bizarre, unbelievably anxiety-ridden, codependent marriage with an inanimate object, and you're scared to leave your house because, "What if it rings?" What if they finally call and tell you they like it or they don't?

Scott Rosenberg: You can't count on anything, and you'll make yourself sick if you do. Anything that happens is gravy, and you should just feel happy to be part of this crazy business. A long time ago, my father said, "Do whatever you want to do, go after it with all your heart, then figure out a way to get paid for it." It's so easy to look at others who are doing better than you, and have this "grass is greener on the other side" attitude that's so endemic to this business. There's a lot of envy in this town, especially among screenwriters. I just say, be happy you're making a living at something you love to do and essentially living your dream.

Terry Rossio: There's almost no way to convey to someone outside the industry the sheer number of projects out there, all of them chasing a very small number of open slots for production. Imagine the Rose Bowl filled with a hundred thousand people trying to get their projects made. And each year, Hollywood will call out the names of maybe forty or fifty people. In that scenario, everything about your project has to be exceptional, from concept through execution.

Michael Schiffer: This business is unbelievably and heartbreakingly slow, and often, when you think a script is done, it's years before it's fully realized. There are hundreds of films, now considered classics, that have taken close to ten years to reach the screen. I think it's because there's an incredible friction between art and commerce, between a piece of work everyone loves and recognizes as great, and a million ways to ask the question, "Will I make my money back if I make this movie?" They can love the script but still pass on it, and then some day, where either the times have changed or the world feels different, someone reads the script and they do see a potential for profit.

As a producer, I try to option material for the longest possible term because it's unrealistic to believe you can set up a movie quickly in this town. Everyone's afraid to commit to anything that's financially doubtful.

CHAPTER 21

PERSEVERANCE

92. Handle Rejection

> *What we call failure is not the falling down,*
> *but the staying down.*
> —MARY PICKFORD

In Hollywood, rejection is a way of life, and writers quickly develop a thicker skin. It helps to understand that the whole business is built on subjective opinions and tastes. Not everyone will like everything. Sure, it always hurts when one doesn't like what you've written, but don't mourn for too long. You just have to persist until you find those who share your vision. When one person rejects you, there are a thousand more to go after. After all, you only need one "yes" to start your career. As the Japanese like to say, "Fall seven times, stand up eight."

Ron Bass: I handle rejection terribly, but not with anger at the other person. I try to realize that anger is an expression of your own insecurity, that the person is rejecting you not to hurt your feelings, but because they don't like what you're doing. So I don't feel terribly angry, more like hurt and insecure and sad. But I have to go home and start working again, and it eventually wears off, especially when you have multiple projects. That's why it's a good habit to have several projects at the same time because when one is going badly, there's still a chance that the others could be doing all right.

Michael Brandt: We learned a long time ago that rejection has to do with so many factors that are out of your control. We'll get fired off a project one day and then hired by the same studio and producers the next day on something else.

Derek Haas: Or we'll get hired right back on to the project from which we were fired. You just have to do the best work you can do and let the chips fall where they may. This business has so many highs and lows—sometimes on the same day. You can't get too up or down about any of it.

Gerald DiPego: You have to believe in yourself and in your idea. You have to know that not everyone will like everything, but it still hurts when they don't. If it doesn't hurt, maybe you don't care enough. You want people to embrace your work. You can't shrug it off. So you just have to get through the disappointment and go on. I've been doing this for almost forty years, so when I put my hopes on a project and the bad news comes, I mourn it no more than a few days and move on.

Tony Gilroy: First, I try to get the pass quickly. A pass is a pass and you could torture yourself with digging around why. But for me, the "why" doesn't concern me. Just tell me "no" quickly. It's no fun to wait around six months for an answer. Now, a pass or a film bombing or getting a bad review is always a disappointment. My father once told me to always embrace it, get it in all the way, don't try to shake it off. Let it in fast and let it hurt. Don't pretend it doesn't bother you. Don't try to deflect it. Absorb how painful it is for as little time as possible. That's what I try to aspire to.

Akiva Goldsman: I used to handle rejection poorly and get depressed. I'd climb on a bed under a blanket and go through a fugue of self-pity that generally would last a couple of days. Now, I wait. What I've learned about moods is that they pass. It's okay to feel sad, it's okay to feel loss and hurt over it. You have to mourn things. If you wrote something and put real energy into it and it doesn't work, you have to dignify that by regretting its loss. Mourn it. You'll be a better writer. If anything, it will redouble your efforts to be good. I wish I were more like the guy who says, "It's good, they're wrong." But I'm the other guy. I generally think the script is terrible, and then I'm surprised when they like it.

Laeta Kalogridis: When things knock you down, you just get back up. I center myself in my family, my kids and spouse and friends, so that work is something I do, not who I am.

Nicholas Kazan: Successful writers have an overwhelming determination, and an ability to accept pain, humiliation, and rejection, and to persevere in the face of towering evidence of lack of talent. (I don't mean that good screenwriters have no talent. Just that screenwriting requires diligence, and until you are good, you are bad, often very bad, and that may appear to be lack of talent.) The easiest way to handle rejection is to take out a contract on the people who rejected you, but that's expensive and risky. Seriously, it's always shocking when people don't like something. The fact is, you don't need every executive in town to love your screenplay. You only need one person at the right level, with the right degree of confidence and courage to champion your work.

But how do you know when to stop, and when to keep going? If you can read your script after it's been rejected a hundred times, and it still reads great, keep going. If it doesn't, you've got to be honest with yourself and believe that maybe they're right, maybe it's ordinary. So you forget about it and try to write an extraordinary screenplay, something you love, that's unusual and different that will set you apart from other people.

Jim Kouf: I don't worry about it too much. That's one good thing about having several projects going on at the same time. When one door closes, you jump to another open door. The same goes even if your movie gets made. The public is either going to love it or reject it; some critics will love you, and some will hate your guts. You've got to have a thick skin in this town because one way or another, everyone will comment on what you do. What else are you going to do? You can't become a writer and not have to deal with people's comments.

Andrew W. Marlowe: You have to learn that failing is part of the process. Execs are paid to say no, and you're asking them to invest a lot of money in something when they don't know how it's going to turn out. You're basically saying to them, "Look, this is a roulette wheel and I'm number eight, and I want you to put $80,000 (WGA minimum scale) on number eight in the hopes that it will turn out."

That's a lot of money in any business. Would you pay yourself $80,000 in the hopes you get a financial return on it? Until you get a track record, you're going to hear a lot of no's. But the trick is to listen to the kind of no's you're getting. Because there are no's that come with encouragement, like, "It was a good story and you're a good writer." That's a version of a yes in this business: "Yes, we can do business together in the future. Maybe if I have a script that needs rewriting, I'll hire you because you have a great original voice." Those are the good kind of no's. Now, if you keep getting, "No, don't waste our time, we never want to see you again," then you need to recalibrate and keep honing your craft until people respond positively to your writing.

Bill Marsilii: I'm developing a thicker skin as I go on. When you work on a project that doesn't become a movie or that comes very close, you have to allow yourself to grieve a bit. But you can't go on too long feeling devastated and never writing again. The best way to get past it is to fall in love again with something else. As a professional, you always have several projects in various stages of development. The more stuff you're excited about, the less painful it gets when one of them dies. There's this great moment in *Ed Wood,* where Johnny Depp is on the phone talking to a studio executive, with this huge smile on his face: "So, what did you think of my movie? . . . Worst movie you ever saw? . . . Well, my next one will be better. . . . Hello?" And this whole time, his smile never flinches. As upsetting as it can get, sometimes you just have to move on and say, "My next one will be better."

Aline Brosh McKenna: Rejection doesn't just happen for projects. It happens everywhere in life, so I deal with it the way I tell my kids how to deal with it. I tell them even the highest paid baseball players miss more times than they hit the ball. But you're in a creative endeavor, and sometimes people don't love your work, but for some reason I got comfortable with it really early. Some people will be your fans and love your work and help you succeed, and others won't. That's just endemic to the job.

Scott Rosenberg: Rejection happens all the time, but my philosophy is that I feel bad for the person who rejected me. But again, it depends on the project. I have this one script I love. It's the best script I ever wrote, and it's amazing that nobody likes it. I can't get this movie made. So when I hear the next person or the next star turns it down, my attitude is, "You poor bastard, do you know what you're doing to your career?" So you basically shift attitudes. I also have bad scripts that get rejected, but I recognize they're bad.

So you deal with it one of two ways—either my material isn't good anyway and I can understand why you're rejecting it and it's okay, or the material is so good that if you're rejecting it, it's your loss. When you first start out and you get rejected left and right, self-doubt can creep in. It's easy to ask yourself, "My God, what am I doing?"

But the great thing about this business is that when one person rejects you, there are a thousand other people to go after. If one agent rejects you, there are many other agencies. And even if all the agencies reject you, guess what? There's a whole other level to explore. They're called producers. And if *all* the producers reject your script, then it's got to be really bad. But then the best part is that you can write another script, and then another. So the numbers are in your favor. Unless you have some serious personal rejection issues, you can always start again with something better.

Terry Rossio: My strategy is to be involved in multiple projects. When one goes bad, you move on to the other. It's also good to work in various media, some of which can be more easily controlled. If a film project goes south, then I have my novel, my play, my graphic novel, etcetera.

Michael Schiffer: I have a twenty-four-hour rule—I tell myself no one is allowed to make me feel miserable for more than one day. Rejection sucks and failure hurts. Anybody who tells you it doesn't is crazy. But if you're letting it go on too long, then you're the loser. If you get hit, you go down, but you can't stay down. You have to get up, pick yourself up and start something new. It's like boxing. The referee is counting to ten. If you stay down, the fight is over.

Tom Schulman: Rejection is painful and it's a shock every time. In order to be good at what you do, you have to be enthusiastic about your writing, so when people read it and they don't like it, it hurts. But I found that, over the years, I've gotten over it faster and faster. The first set of rejections probably took me days. Eventually, I got to the point where I'd lie down on the floor for about fifteen minutes. I'd think for the first five minutes, "I'm through, I'm out, I've got to find something else to do, I can't take it, blah, blah, blah." And then five minutes of, "What else am I gonna do?" And then five minutes of, "What can I do to make this better?"

Ed Solomon: It's a very fine line because you need to believe in yourself and keep pushing, but sometimes your stuff just isn't good enough. So how do you know? You have to really look into your gut. There's a difference between hearing creative criticism and getting abject rejection. If you get a rejection and people are saying, "It's not for me," you say, "Fine, it works for me." But if they're saying, "I just don't find the central character worth following," and someone else says, "I have trouble liking your central character," then you need to look at it. Be very aware of the kind of rejection you get. Some of it is good, because it tells you something isn't working.

93. Finish What You Start

> *Never regret. If it's good, it's wonderful.*
> *If it's bad, it's experience.*
> —VICTORIA HOLT

With few exceptions, you'll need to write several spec screenplays before you reach that high standard of craft demanded by the industry. Unlike many aspiring writers who become psychologically paralyzed and quit after writing the first twenty or thirty pages, successful screenwriters finish what they start because they believe in it and aren't afraid to fail. Each script is a learning experience.

Scott Rosenberg: It's very important to finish what you start. I remember a professor who showed me a drawer full of scripts, seventy-five sets of the first twenty pages. He wrote the first twenty pages of seventy-five different screenplays and went no further. This paralyzed me. Even if I just start something that sucks and is wildly uncommercial, or an exact movie comes out and I know I'll never sell it, I'll still finish it. Every script you finish, you learn.

Eric Roth: The most important thing is to finish what you start, even if it takes forever or it's painful. There are no secrets, no mystery. Some people are better at it than others. Some have different things to say, but finishing is the key.

Michael Schiffer: The act of finishing something is absolutely critical. People who say they wish they'd make themselves write, or that they'd write more if they had more time, are not writers. If you don't write, you're not a writer. Every writer I know is incredibly hard working. They work their tails off every day. How are you going to compete unless you do the same? The only chance to break in is to outwork the competition and never give up. If I had an impulse for a story, any story idea that seemed to have a beginning, middle, and end, and some sort of commercial appeal, rather than play Hamlet and wonder, "Should I write this, should I not," I'd sit down and write the story and see where it took me. I'd make myself finish it. I did this over and over until I finally got a strong writing sample that opened the doors for *Colors*.

94. Don't Give Up Easily

Sticking to it is the genius.
—Thomas Edison

There's an old folktale about a young woman who wanted to be a dancer. One day she learned that the greatest dancing teacher of all time was to pass through her small town, so she practiced and practiced in the hope she could impress him. When the day arrived, she managed to be introduced to him and she asked, "Oh, wise teacher, would you tell me if I have what it takes to be a great dancer?" The man asked her to dance for him, and she danced like she'd never danced before. It was her greatest performance yet. But, unimpressed after only thirty seconds, the man said she didn't have the talent, and that she should quit. Devastated, the young woman ran to her home in tears, threw her dancing shoes in a trunk, and forgot about being a dancer. She got married, became a housewife with children, and led a happy life for twenty years, until she had a chance meeting with the same dancing teacher. She couldn't help asking him how he knew within thirty seconds that she didn't have it. He responded, "I couldn't tell, but if you quit so easily because I told you to, then you weren't a real dancer."

Bottom line: if you're passionate about your goal, nothing will stand in your way—no naysayers, no statistics, no experts. If someone tells you you'll never make it, if they try talking you out of it by listing all the logical reasons you should quit, you keep going, more determined than ever, because you love it and it has meaning to you. As Marianne Williamson says, "If you want to give up, then perhaps you should give up. The real writer doesn't consider that an option. Courage matters as much as talent." So when should you stop trying? If you're doing this because you love it, then you should quit when you're no longer having any fun. When you've done the best you could and the process just brings you more depression than joy, you should re-evaluate your goals (see next habit).

Akiva Goldsman: Just truly persevere. It's so frightening how many wonderful writers stopped writing because they couldn't take the pain of rejection. Great writers are just stubborn. There's a persistence of vision over time, because being a writer is a life led. It's not about having written a single thing. A writer writes. Everyone says it. It's true. A writer spends a life writing. And if that's what you must do for a living, then you will. If it's just fantasy and the rejection knocks you out, then it should, because it's not work for the squeamish.

Nicholas Kazan: I wrote a play in college that a professor gave to a theater director, and we never heard back from the guy. Months went by and I just assumed he didn't like it. I was depressed and didn't think any more of it. The professor later ran into the same director again and asked him what he thought of the play. He said he didn't remember it, that he probably lost it, and to send it to him again. So the professor did; the director liked it and he ended up producing it and a number of my other plays. This is a case where the writer's psychology, which is to be timid in the face of the world, to be paranoid, to see rejection everywhere and be emotionally infected by it, all of these worked against me. Had I not had this persistent advocate, my plays would never have been done.

It's like Faulkner, who showed *The Sound and the Fury* to every publisher in New York and nobody would publish it. Likewise, you could show your script to a hundred people and it could be great. There's always one hundred and one. But if a lot of them tell you it doesn't work, maybe you should go back home, because all that may be waiting for you here is frustration, rejection, and heartache. Certainly, these things are waiting for you even if you're a success, but if rejection is your sole diet, it can be very difficult. I wrote fifteen scripts before I sold my first one.

Jim Kouf: I don't think you can ever give up, because the older you become, the wiser and better you become. There are many instances, though less true in Hollywood, of people making it later in life. You never know. If you really love doing it, you ought to keep doing it, and if you're truly talented, you'll probably get discovered. You can always *not* do it, then you know for sure what the outcome is.

Scott Rosenberg: The best quote I ever saw was from Steven Soderbergh, where he felt that luck equaled talent plus perseverance. And I really believe that's true, because you can be super-talented, but if you're not willing to really gut it out for a long time, you'll have a difficult time. I have friends who were wildly talented writers when I first got here, and after two or three years they were like, "You know what? I want to get married, I want to have a family, I can't deal with this anymore." Now they're selling computers.

I remember watching an episode of *Taxi* where the actor character says, "If I don't make it by my thirtieth birthday, I'm quitting." I had that in the back of my head. But the actor in *Taxi* doesn't quit on his thirtieth birthday, he just tacks on another five years. The problem for me was, what else was I going to do? IBM wasn't going to hire me. You have to believe in yourself and in the process, and have a strong support system around you. I was lucky that no one, not even my parents or my girlfriend, ever said to me, "Why are you wasting your time when you could become a lawyer or something?" or "Stop loafing around. I hear there's a cashier opening at Wal-Mart." They were always completely supportive.

Michael Schiffer: I came to town and gave myself a five-year plan. I had written hard for five years with no sales, then I came out here when I was thirty-five and said, "I'm going to work every day, all day, and I'm not going to look back once for five years. And if I haven't broken into the business by the time I'm forty, I'll just get a day job, I'll quit, walk away from it, become a teacher somewhere, or find a job in business."

But for five years, I wasn't going to second-guess myself. I wasn't going to fail for lack of hard work or effort, so I worked really hard for that time, and I wrote fourteen scripts in three years before I got *Colors*. Sure, they weren't all good, but I made myself write everything from beginning to end, and forced myself to rewrite everything at least once.

Ed Solomon: I was very lucky to somehow land a job when I was a senior in college, but I almost gave up once, right before we sold *Bill and Ted*. I had gone about a year and a half without working after my first job, and I thought the script was funny, but my agents wouldn't send it out, so I finally left them. I walked out of the agency with no agents and no deal. Then, I began to think maybe they were right, maybe the script was no good. And at my lowest moment, we found someone who believed in it and got it set up.

95. Change What Doesn't Work

> *I can't control the wind, but I can adjust my sails.*
>
> —Anonymous

There's a saying that insanity is doing the same thing over and over and expecting different results. As an aspiring writer, persistence is good, but you must also have the flexibility to change what doesn't work. Different actions lead to different results. Successful screenwriters adapt to failures and learn from their mistakes. Their attitude is, "There is definitely a way, and I'll try different routes until I get there."

Thomas Edison is known as one of the most persistent scientists, perfecting the light bulb after one thousand tries. When asked why he kept going after 999 failures, he responded, "They weren't failures, just 999 ways not to invent a light bulb. Every wrong attempt discarded was another step forward."

Leslie Dixon: I woke up one morning really bored with what I was doing, and decided to do a dramatic book adaptation on spec. It was a book in the public domain that I've always liked, and it wasn't a comedy at all. I sold it, got *The Thomas Crown Affair* off of it, which was also not a comedy. Sometimes, you've got to shake up the way you work from time to time and try different methods. For the adaptation, I started doing more research because it demanded it, but I didn't use an outline. I tried to go in more by my gut and my unconscious. I realized that was a new resource I hadn't really jacked into, like I've spent all those years writing from the front part of my brain and not really relaxing, letting things pop into my mind more.

Your subconscious is a very valuable ally. It can solve problems without driving you insane. So suddenly, my habits changed—the hours I worked, the way I worked—and I was pleased not only with the results but with the reaction to the results. I also had no idea I could write a genre other than comedy. It was a revelation that got me all excited to be in the business again. I really believe I'm a better drama writer than a comedy writer, and I never knew that. So changing your routines once in a while can be a good thing.

96. Re-evaluate Your Goals Regularly

A job is what we do for money; work is what we do for love.
—MARYSARAH QUINN

Although there's something admirable in the stubborn refusal to take no for an answer, at some point you have to re-evaluate your goals. There are people who've struggled for over twenty years without even a positive comment on their work, and who are bitter and jaded by their experiences. When it's clear that screenwriting brings them more depression than joy, you wonder about their choices. The demarcation line should be in the joy of the artistic pursuit despite the temporary setbacks. Every so often, take a moment to ask yourself, "Am I having fun trying to make it? Am I doing my best? Do I still love writing screenplays?" If you answer "no" to all these questions, maybe you should re-evaluate your aspirations, and focus on what you truly love to do.

Gerald DiPego: It's hard to discourage people, because you want them to follow their dreams. But it goes back to getting that feedback from people you trust. If the feedback keeps coming in more negative than positive, if you haven't broken through, or if nobody is embracing your work, it has to tell you something. You can persevere and take more classes and try to get better, but if you don't see the improvement, it's a big indicator you need to re-evaluate your goals.

Nicholas Kazan: If you feel you must write, and your real triumph is reaching the end of a screenplay, keep at it. But if you're making up your screenplays and people don't respond, if you don't take joy in it, if the act of writing movies doesn't transport you, quit. If you're not getting the compensatory joys and satisfaction out of the process itself, then it's too difficult.

CHAPTER 22

PASSION

97. Pay the Price

> *Success is simple. First, you decide what you want*
> *specifically; second, you decide you're willing to pay the price*
> *to make it happen, and then, you pay that price.*
> —BUNKER HUNT

Think of the life you'd live if you weren't pursuing this silly dream of becoming a screenwriter—going out with friends, dating, getting married, having children, traveling—in other words, a *normal* life. If this seems more attractive to you than years of starving, struggling, and honing your craft, quit now. Because you have to be willing to pay the price of entry into Screenwriting Land. Frank Darabont speaks from experience when he says, "There are potentially more talented writers and directors than I, working in shoe stores and Burger Kings across the nation; the difference is I was willing to put in the nine years of effort and they weren't."

Sure, there are exceptions, with first-timers gaining entry with their first script. But the general consensus is that the journey to professional screenwriting will take time and effort, money, obsessive personal involvement, diligent follow-through, constant rejection, personal pain, social sacrifice, and a persistent belief in yourself, no matter how overwhelming the obstacles. Are you prepared to pay the price?

Gerald DiPego: To me, writing is very close to an obsession. Those who are serious about it are driven, so paying the price goes with the territory. You'll have obstacles and disappointments, and if you hit those and you give up and walk away, then maybe you weren't as driven, as inspired, or as obsessed to begin with. And that's not a bad thing because you learn how much you can take.

Jim Kouf: There's no other way. And there's no guarantee that any particular way will be successful. Everyone has to find their own way into this business. It's not like you can go and apply for a screenwriting job. You have to write something that's good enough that people want to buy, and at that point, if the script is good enough, they'll ask you, "What else do you have?" or "We'd like you to rewrite this script," or "What ideas do you have?" But until then, you're paying those dues, and there's no guarantee you'll ever break into this business. And even if you do, there's no guarantee that you'll ever sell another script. So you really need to have the talent and the desire, but it's not as if you can tell people how good you are. You have to let other people tell you how good you are. I could think I'm the greatest writer in the world, but it doesn't matter what I think. What matters is what everyone else thinks, and what I can deliver on the page.

Scott Rosenberg: I wrote ten scripts before I got my first agent, wrote another two before my first sale and another three before anything got made. That's the most important advice I could give to anyone starting out: Write a lot of scripts. I get this phone call at least once a month: "Hi, my mother met your mother at a wedding and I just graduated college, and I'm out here, and I really like your work, and I wrote a script, and I'll be happy if you would read it." And I say, "Okay, how many scripts have you written?" and they say this is their first. "Are you sure you want me to read it? Because I'm very busy. I'd be happy to read your script, but if it blows, which it will because it's a first script, I'll never read another one." I look back at all these ten scripts I wrote, and they suck. Sure, they have moments of great stuff, but who am I at age twenty-two to think I'm going to write the Great American Screenplay? It's just wrong. I didn't have the life experience, and I was just learning to crawl, learning my process. And these kids, with their lottery mentality, think they just wrote *The Terminator*, and it's ridiculous. The one thing I'm most proud of in my process is that I was always writing. When people talk to me about "paying your dues," and I think about these lean years when I had no money, I was sharing a room, sleeping on mattresses on the floor, driving the worst car, working in the worst jobs, it didn't feel like I was paying my dues. I was still living my life, going to the movies and having a girlfriend and watching sports, and all of a sudden, I look back at those years and I realize I was living like an animal. But there was a kind of innocence to that time that I long for.

Tom Schulman: There are two kinds of dues you have to pay, before and after you make it as a professional writer. So you're always paying your dues. If you continue to write and your output is high, you begin to think your writing is of good quality only to be demoralized and frustrated by the system. It's unlike any other professional system where if you start at the bottom and if you do good work, you progress up the ladder. In Hollywood, there is no ladder, no merit system. You could be completely out of it one day and on top of the system the next. There's no common apprenticeship with low-paying wages that graduates to an assistantship with higher wages, which graduates to a professorship with full tenure. The frustrating part is that you really don't know if you'll ever make a living at it. It could be one year, twenty years, or never. You just try to get better at it and hope you'll catch a break.

98. Be Honest with Yourself

A writer knows he's a writer.
—John Barth

What would you do if money were no longer an issue? Be honest with yourself. You have nothing to lose and everything to gain. Imagine you just won the Mega Powerball lottery, the biggest jackpot in history. What will you do to occupy your time after you've bought all the cars and houses and traveled around the world? Whatever you see yourself doing every day with excitement is what you should be doing right now. Life is too short to spend it struggling to break into a highly competitive career you're not really passionate about.

Ron Bass: Do you really love writing? If you can't answer this question honestly, then you're in the wrong business, because the only thing that can sustain a screenwriter through the assault the movie business puts on you, all the unimaginably deflating, rejecting, humiliating experiences, even with all its good intentions, is that you *love* to do it. People who become writers because they want to *be* writers are dead meat. If what you want are the trappings of it, if you like to *think* of yourself as a writer, an artist in your own eyes, because it gives you an inflated feeling of self-worth, or if you think you'll get rich doing it, get fame and praise, go to parties and hang out with beautiful actresses and famous directors all day long, the only bad part of this is that you actually have to write the stuff. Sure, you may live through the writing part and you'll be a writer, but if that's where you're coming from, don't even start. If you don't have that drive, I don't know what else could see you through. Maybe if you thought you had a gift for it and you were incredibly greedy, that greed could drive through the slings and arrows. I've yet to meet a really great writer whom I respect who hates to write and just does it because it's a way to earn a living. Sure, I've known many writers who felt burned out and became directors. They just got tired of writing; their flame went out. But they still had their skill and craft to still write and support themselves between directing jobs, because it's the only thing they knew how to do.

Amy Holden Jones: It's common knowledge that people who persevere are more likely to succeed. On the other hand, I know an awful lot of people who persevered when they didn't have the talent. So it's very important to find out whether you have the talent first. If you're a screenwriter, you should have a backup plan because the rate of failure is so high. You have to be willing to do something else if this doesn't work. I think it was Tom Schulman who once said, "Most screenwriters don't fail, they just quit." Unfortunately, half the time, they're right to quit. It's a very difficult line. There are a million good reasons to quit. Go start an Internet company, be your own boss, write a novel. This isn't a good way to make a living. You can make a lot more money learning about stocks than writing screenplays, and if you care deeply about your own work, it's emotionally difficult when they massacre your work and take it away from you. I stayed because I was successful at it. Part of life is finding out what you're good at and sticking with it, so figure out first if you're good at writing screenplays, and then if you can handle the frustrations.

Nicholas Kazan: I was a speaker at a conference and I said, "Take your registration form, go back out there and get your money back," and they all laughed. But I told them I was very serious, that if they even thought of following my advice, they'd never make it. You have to believe in yourself and persevere even in the face of massive evidence to the contrary, because sometimes people make leaps in their writing. I know I did, several times, and I couldn't have anticipated these leaps. Your work *can* get better, but it doesn't happen for everybody. There are people who *should* go back home. The trick is knowing which category you fall into. Are you someone with talent who'll make it eventually? Or are you the one who'll work at it for twenty years and never make it?

Scott Rosenberg: To a certain extent, you know if you have it. People aren't stupid. Read other scripts and then read your own. Unless you're completely blind, you can tell if your writing meets that high standard needed to get attention in this town. All my jobs, when I had no money, were crappy jobs. The minute I punched the clock at five, I never thought about them again until the next day, because my writing was priority number one. I think that people who take real jobs that consume them beyond that eight-hour day know at some level that they don't really have it. They're consciously, or unconsciously, hedging their bets. Whereas the people who go for broke are so confident and passionate, they always know that if they do their best in this business, they'll eventually make it.

99. Remain Passionate Despite the Disappointments

A successful man is one who can lay a firm foundation
with the bricks that others throw at him.
—David Brinkley

After reading about the downside of being a screenwriter in Hollywood—how even highly successful screenwriters are disrespected and mistreated, how difficult writing a good screenplay actually is, the horrors of dealing with the Hollywood system, and the sacrifices needed to eventually make it—you have to wonder what could possibly motivate our mentors to keep going despite these frustrations. Here's a hint: It starts with a P and rhymes with "fashion."

Akiva Goldsman: This is what I do for a living. I like it and hate it the same way someone at IBM hates it. If I were at IBM, I'd be having my own set of challenges and rewards and I'd be engaged in them because that's my job. It doesn't mean I don't hate it sometimes, and that I don't fantasize about leaving it all behind one day. What it means is that I actually get to do what I want for a living, and there's a difference between that and loving every second of it.

Amy Holden Jones: It's the one thing I do well, and at regular intervals movies have been made from my works. If they weren't, I probably would have given up. I know writers who have written a number of interesting scripts that never got made and I understand when they feel like quitting after a while.

Aline Brosh McKenna: We work for other entities, so we don't have the luxury to dictate how things should go. The only thing you control 100 percent is what you get to do alone in your writing cave. So it's best to focus all your energies on the stuff you can control and don't be affected by the stuff you can't. I read about another writer who had a piece of paper above her desk that said, "Write with no attachment to the outcome." If you obsess about what's selling right now, or what so-and-so will think of this, or who got that assignment, you'll be crippled.

Terry Rossio: About one out of every seven movies I've worked on ends with a group of people in power (director, star, producer, studio) who get the story and respect the screenplay. Everyone is on the same page, so to speak, and the film comes out better than I could ever imagine, due to the combined talents of the group. You live for that scenario. That makes it all worthwhile.

Eric Roth: You have daily frustrations with any kind of work you do. You may write a scene that just doesn't work, but the upside is that you have stories where it does work, and some wonderful discoveries where you sort of thrill yourself because it's just you and the work at that point. Then, once you turn it in, there's a whole different world that enters into it. What's exciting is working with directors who have the same vision, and that can be fun and stimulating. I also enjoy when we do a table reading of it because there's a sense that something is really there and that it's playing the way you envisioned it. It's very pure, there's no ego involved; we can strike and change lines that don't work. And then, there's the thrill when the movie works and when you're on the set during production. But at some point, you have to let it go because it's not yours anymore.

Michael Schiffer: When I'm working, I try to do the best I can so that there are never any regrets. If I work as hard as I can and give my best, I never feel that if I worked a little harder, this wouldn't have happened. By the time I turn it in, I have taken it as far as I can take it, and then I just move on. You've got to have a life of your own. The longer I'm at this, the more I feel like the business can't be the only definition of your soul.

Tom Schulman: What keeps me going is the passion for whatever I'm writing. Despite the terrible things that happen to my various projects in development, the one I'm working on is the baby in the womb with the hope it'll someday be a genius. It's what keeps me excited and makes it worth getting up in the morning.

Robin Swicord: There is a sense of mission. In a sense, I feel very lucky that I knew early on I was a storyteller, and it's the one thing I've come here to do. I know that at the most basic level, these frustrations can't really reach me, because where I really live is not available to them.

100. Don't Take It Too Seriously

> *I shall live badly if I do not write,*
> *and I shall write badly if I do not live.*
> —Françoise Sagan

When breaking into the industry demands such a high level of effort, sacrifice, and obsession, when aspiring screenwriters must give the craft every fiber of their being and think, eat, sleep, and breathe screenwriting twenty-four hours a day without a guarantee they'll ever make it, it's difficult to say, "Don't take it too seriously."

But screenwriting shouldn't be *everything* that you're about as a human being. If you're single, with no responsibilities, feel free to be as obsessed as you want to be, while still balancing your life (Habit 47). But if you have meaningful relationships, a family, children depending on your being there, you have to realize what's important and act accordingly. Never sacrifice your loved ones for a screenplay. Successful screenwriters aren't as obsessed as you'd think. But they still take their professionalism and the attached responsibilities, such as delivering quality work on time, seriously. As Henry Miller once said, "Develop interest in life as you see it—in people, things, literature, music. The world is so rich, simply throbbing with rich pleasures, beautiful souls, and interesting people. Forget yourself." Simply remember this: There's screenwriting and there's life. Making the distinction will make you a better writer.

Gerald DiPego: You have to be somewhat serious, because writing is an obsession. You're so passionate about it, it's something you have to do, even if you're not getting paid for it. But it's a lot healthier if it's not all that you're about. In fact, you'll probably be better at your writing if it isn't all that you're about. A wider life makes you a fuller person and enables you to see the world outside yourself. If you're so wrapped up in your craft, it becomes too self-involving and you're not really living in the world anymore.

Bill Marsilii: I have found that the quality of my day-to-day living has become far more important to me than it used to be, and much more important than career success, where if I'd made certain career choices, I'd be missing out on my home life and my daughter's youth. I feel blessed that I can come out in the middle of my workday and play with my daughter in the backyard, when there are kings and presidents and CEOs who can't do that.

Michael Schiffer: Young writers tend to be more obsessive. Writing is everything to them, twenty hours a day, and it has to be, in order to get somewhere. But when you have a family, you try to get home and make your family the most important thing in your life. It's such a different universe at home, that you have to shut off all the writing anxieties. It's a discipline that's important to cultivate as a human being. You can't possibly have good relationships if you walk around brooding about stuff all the time.

Ed Solomon: Everything in this town plays into the easy buttons that get pushed and take people off their path—greed, power, glamour, sex, fame. It actually takes more work in this business to stay clear of that. I do the same thing—write—whether I'm paid or not, and I like writing. Ultimately, it all comes down to the work. It's not that I'm really passionate about writing. It's just that I'm far less passionate about driving a bread truck. What's worth taking really seriously? At best, we provide a diversion for people. On rare occasions, we make something that has some value. As an entire media, we definitely have an effect, but nothing we do is worth taking that seriously. Self-importance is the death of creativity. Maybe it's important to express yourself and be heard, but when you start believing you need to make noise because others need to hear you, you're on the road to ruin.

CHAPTER 23

PRACTICE

101. Write No Matter What

*Writing energy is like anything else:
the more you put in, the more you get out.*
—RICHARD REEVES

There's this joke about an old man who walks into a piano store, sits down at a piano, and starts playing. But he's really awful. "I don't understand," says the old man, puzzled, "I've been listening to Mozart for thirty years!"

You may think you could write a movie because you've been watching movies all your life. Putting words on the page is the easy part. Engaging a reader with these words is another story. Hemingway once said a writer must write a million words before he can call himself a writer. It's like any other activity—playing a sport, learning a musical instrument, or mastering the craft of writing. You've got to do it regularly to become any good at it. Practice makes perfect.

Michael Brandt: It helps to keep working on multiple things so you aren't so invested into one script or one person's decision. As soon as you finish a spec, start writing another. Wake up each day and say, "No one is going to work harder at this than me today."

Jim Kouf: I had the usual beginner's frustrations, like "How come they're not buying this?" I did a lot of writing, figuring it out on my own, because I didn't go to film school. I wrote eleven TV specs before

I got someone to take me seriously, then it took six feature scripts before I wrote one that was good enough.

Aline Brosh McKenna: What's hard for writers is that you're in the hopes and dreams business, so if things don't go the way you'd hoped, it feels more personal. But it's a craft and it's a collaboration, and I encourage people to put more boats in the water and just keep writing scripts until you find the right environment. "Writers write," as my agent used to say.

Michael Schiffer: Developing craft is a very slow process. If you were playing the violin, you wouldn't expect to pick it up, then go to Carnegie Hall within six months. And yet, people expect their first or second script to sell and become a hit movie. It's a bit delusional. Sure, there may be instances of this happening, but generally, it's a craft that takes the requisite five to twenty years to develop.

Tom Schulman: We all hear the stories of overnight successes. But almost every one of these successes will tell you that it was an overnight success that took ten to twenty years. This is by far the rule.

CONCLUSION

FADE OUT

Do not seek to follow in the footsteps of the wise;
seek what they sought.

—Matsuo Basho

Well, there you have it, 101 habits to model in your training run to become the next great screenwriter. Our mentors want to congratulate you for being such an attentive apprentice and leave you with some final words of wisdom.

Ron Bass: If I have to narrow any advice down to a sound bite, I'd say write every day, only write if you love it, prepare your stories in advance, don't rewrite your own material unless someone is paying you to do it, read other people's stuff, retain the humility that you're not the world's best expert who has all the answers, let it hurt when rejected but don't get hardened against it, keep writing new things, new genres, as different as you can, different characters, different situations. You build your instrument. It's like working with weights. You only get better as you do it. Just keep doing it.

Steven de Souza: Despite all the frustrations, at the end of the day nothing really matters except the writing. It must be a lot tougher for a director or a star when a movie falls apart than for a writer, because if a producer is not interested, you can go to the next one, and if a few turn you down, forget the producers and write the damn thing. All you need is a pen and piece of paper. Screw the Pentium III and the screenwriting software. Go off by yourself and write a killer script that will show that everybody else is wrong, will start a new trend, and make you every struggling writer's new hero.

Gerald DiPego: Always do the very best work you can. Don't rush it. Be as open as you can to feedback. Believe in your work. If it touches you in some deep way, then trust that there are other people out there who will feel the same.

Leslie Dixon: No matter what you do, you have to get an agent. It's like the old real estate maxim: "Agent, agent, agent."

Tony Gilroy: You gotta love the actual craft of putting words together in a row that affect a reader emotionally. If you care about doing good work, you gotta care about the reader. I love making a script a lot better that it has to be in terms of its prose. That level of quality control is what keeps me interested and puts my ass on the chair. Take the time to rewrite your descriptions. Take pride in your narrative prose. Tell yourself that there's no release until your prose is perfect, until the reader can see the movie that you want them to see.

Akiva Goldsman: Bruce Beresford taught me something wonderful. He taught me that everyone is really twelve years old. Everyone thinks they're a kid in a grownup's body, and if you remember this, you stop being scared because, just as I'm scared of being found out, so is the big director across the way and so is the big actor around the corner. Knowing that we are still in our hearts the kids we were, doing our best to wear grownup clothes, helps us walk a little easier through the world.

Derek Haas: It's okay to break the rules. Also, watch as many films and read as many screenplays as you can. Then find a partner as good as Brandt.

Michael Brandt: Don't write a script, write a movie. We always say, "Forget 'write what you know': write what you think is cool." We just wrote scripts that we wanted to see on screen and hoped someone else would like them.

Amy Holden Jones: Be absolutely certain you really want to do this. I once asked a writer why she wanted to do it and she said she didn't like to write prose and long descriptions but she loved writing scenes and dialogue. That's a good answer, when screenwriting is the type of writing that you love to do. Get realistic about the nature of the business and study it the way you would any other industry. You'll learn this by getting a job in the business, even if it's an unpaid job.

Laeta Kalogridis: *Live within your means.* It's a modern version of having "A Room of One's Own." You can't write if you can't eat and pay the mortgage. Money is a kind of freedom. You have control over how much freedom you have if you're careful how much you spend.

Nicholas Kazan: If you were a carpenter, I guarantee your hundredth desk would be a lot better than your first, just like your twentieth screenplay will be a lot better than your first. Just keep going and make sure you really love what you do. I'm perfectly happy about the specs I wrote that haven't sold. I look at them, I worked hard on them and I'm very proud of them. They're not ruined yet because they exist only in my head. They still have perfect production values and they're beautifully shot with fantastic performances. Maybe they'll get made one day, maybe not. Who cares? I'm happy about them.

Jim Kouf: I don't think you can learn how to write by listening to anybody tell you how to write. I don't know where the muse comes from, or how it's done. You may be able to learn the craft, but how do you teach somebody to be witty? You have to be interested in a lot of stuff and have an almost obsessive compulsive behavior, because you really have to be interested in something to make you want to write about it and spend that much time with it. You have to be able to step back and look at your own work and ask if it's any good. Most of the time, good writing is obvious; it comes alive on the page. But then again, somebody else might hate it, so who the hell knows? But if everybody thinks it's not good, then obviously I've done something wrong. I never believe I'm right above everybody else. That's the kind of script we never send out.

Andrew W. Marlowe: Never be boring on the page. It doesn't mean dazzle me with action or have crazy stuff happening on every page. You have an obligation that your audience be emotionally engaged in whatever story you're telling.

Bill Marsilii: If you want to break in with a spec script, don't settle for the first concept that pops into your mind. It doesn't matter how well you execute it or how may drafts you take it through. If the core idea doesn't rise above the thousands of mediocre ones, and if it doesn't inspire you to rise above thousands of other writers to be the best that you can be, you'll never get on anyone's radar. Ultimately, if the strength of your idea can open so many doors for you, why not find a really good one? Hold out for a soul mate of an idea. If other people love it too, you could end up with a career.

Aline Brosh McKenna: Someone once said to me the equation for good writing is ass plus chair. It's all about sitting down and doing the work.

Scott Rosenberg: At the end of the day, I really believe I have the best job in the world. Every day is different. They pay me a fortune of money. I get to work with heroes I've grown up with. In this crazy, wonderful world, I look at the guy who has to go to the office, sit in a cubicle and punch numbers all day, and I wonder what I would have done if it turned out to be me, and I tremble at it. My life is so far away from that. I wake up every morning not knowing what the day will bring and that's really cool.

Terry Rossio: John McTiernan told us once to never write exposition. Instead, create questions the audience wants answered, and then answer those questions; the information doesn't feel like exposition. John Musker said that complex stories can only be explored in a rudimentary fashion, whereas a simple story can be explored with depth. My writing partner, Ted Elliott, noted that theory is only useful as a diagnostic tool. And one last thing: The most common mistake I see beginners make today is improper assessment of film concepts. Make sure you have a great idea before you commit to writing a full script.

Eric Roth: Finish what you start. Think of it as a journey.

Michael Schiffer: Aim high. Work harder than you think you should. If it's hard work, you're doing it right. If you're writing about the real world, research it. Be relentless in rewriting. Put it out to people and see what their reactions are. If they give you notes, you may not always agree with them, but always try to figure out what is the underlying problem that made them speak up in the first place. Their articulation of the problem may not give you the answer you need, but their need to fix something probably comes from an underlying problem in the script, and you must look beneath the surface to figure out why they were unhappy with this part of the script. If you hand in something utterly brilliant, they'll hand it back to you with stars in their eyes and say, "Wow!"

Tom Schulman: Write what you love. Don't write for the market because who knows what the market wants? The best market is yourself.

Ed Solomon: As best you can, try to find the joy and peace in the process, not in the results, because no matter how successful you become, if what you're looking for are results, you'll be very frustrated. Try to have a balanced life. Nothing we do ultimately matters. The success of *Men in Black* was great and I'm sure it entertained millions, but do we really think the world would be any different if *Men in Black* didn't exist? On the rare occasion you do something that really affects someone, that's great, but what's more important are the people you affect in your daily life. That's where you will leave a mark. People who say, "If my movie touches just one person it will be worthwhile," are kidding themselves. If you're interested in touching one person, go out and spend $200 and pay for a school teacher in an African village for a year. If you're going to waste $100 million and a lot of people's precious time, and be miserable in the process, all you'll do is create a lot more misery.

Robin Swicord: This is more to women who are home writing with children, and it's a topic worthy of a whole new chapter. It's very important to know that it's perfectly fine to say, "This time is for me and for this other work." It teaches children to be self-reliant. They know you're there but merely aloof. They know they're free to set themselves down on the floor with their own games in front of them and make their own little world. You set a good example by doing this and saying, "This work that I do, which is very important to me, I want to do it now. So you go over there and find your thing to do and we'll do it side by side." This is the best thing to do for yourself, because many women feel guilty about stepping apart from the family and doing this other thing they also came here to do. No one ever said this to me, and I just want to say it's a good thing for you and it's good for your kids.

Final Words

The only question in your mind should not be, "How do I break into the business?" but "How can I write a great script that will excite anyone who reads it?" Remember that no matter how successful screenwriters broke into the business, they first wrote a great script that got the attention of a reader. When you finally write that great piece of material, Hollywood will take notice. If your script is genuinely good, agents will find you. This is the one area that no one in the industry will argue against: A great script is the last and final argument. But first, you must develop the right habits, the behaviors, skills, and attitudes to get you there. Try them out. If they work for you, fine. If they don't, develop your own and move on. As Habit 100 says, don't take it too seriously. Relax. *Write*. Play. *Write*. Eat. *Write*. Laugh. *Write*. Love. *Write*. Sleep. Repeat daily as necessary.

Good luck!

INDEX OF HABITS

INDEX OF SCREENWRITERS' PANEL COMMENTS

ABOUT THE AUTHOR

Karl Iglesias is a screenwriter and sought-after script doctor and consultant, specializing in the reader's emotional response to the written page.

He is the author of *Writing for Emotional Impact: Advanced Dramatic Techniques to Attract, Engage, and Fascinate the Reader from Beginning to End,* and a contributor to *Now Write! Screenwriting* (Tarcher/Penguin).

He teaches at UCLA Extension Writers' Program, where he was named Outstanding Instructor in Screenwriting in 2010, and has led workshops at the Screenwriting Expo, the Great American Pitchfest, and online at Writers University.

He's a former story analyst and development executive for various production companies.

He's been profiled in the *Los Angeles Times, Screentalk Magazine, Writer Magazine,* and the television show "Connie Martinson Talks Books."

He holds a psychology degree from Cornell University and an MFA in Creative Writing and Writing for the Performing Arts from UC Riverside-Palm Desert.

He lives in Los Angeles and can be reached through his website at *www.karliglesias.com.*